CONTEMPORARY WRITERS

General Editors
MALCOLM BRADBURY
and
CHRISTOPHER BIGSBY

GRAHAM GREENE

GRAHAM
GREENE

JOHN SPURLING

METHUEN
LONDON AND NEW YORK

First published in 1983 by
Methuen & Co. Ltd
11 New Fetter Lane, London EC4P 4EE
Published in the USA by
Methuen & Co.
in association with Methuen, Inc.
733 Third Avenue, New York, NY 10017

© 1983 John Spurling

Typeset by Rowland Phototypesetting Ltd
Printed in Great Britain by
Richard Clay (The Chaucer Press) Ltd
Bungay, Suffolk

British Library Cataloguing in Publication Data

Spurling, John
Graham Greene.—(Contemporary writers)
1. Greene, Graham—Criticism and interpretation
I. Title   II. Series
823'.912   PR6013.R44Z/

ISBN 0-416-31850-9

Library of Congress Cataloging in Publication Data

Spurling, John, 1936–
Graham Greene.

(Contemporary writers)
Bibliography: P.
1. Greene, Graham, 1904–   —Criticism and interpretation.
I. Title.   II. Series.
PR6013.R44Z86   1983   823'.912   83-13421

ISBN 0-416-31850-9 (pbk.)

CONTENTS

GENERAL EDITORS' PREFACE

The contemporary is a country which we all inhabit, but there is little agreement as to its boundaries or its shape. The serious writer is one of its most sensitive interpreters, but criticism is notoriously cautious in offering a response or making a judgement. Accordingly, this continuing series is an endeavour to look at some of the most important writers of our time, and the questions raised by their work. It is, in effect, an attempt to map the contemporary, to describe its aesthetic and moral topography.

The series came into existence out of two convictions. One was that, despite all the modern pressures on the writer and on literary culture, we live in a major creative time, as vigorous and alive in its distinctive way as any that went before. The other was that, though criticism itself tends to grow more theoretical and apparently indifferent to contemporary creation, there are grounds for a lively aesthetic debate. This series, which includes books written from various standpoints, is meant to provide a forum for that debate. By design, some of those who have contributed are themselves writers, willing to respond to their contemporaries; others are critics who have brought to the discussion of current writing the spirit of contemporary criticism or simply a conviction, forcibly and coherently argued, for the contemporary significance of their subjects. Our aim, as the series develops, is to continue to explore the works of major post-war writers – in fiction, drama and poetry – over an international range, and thereby to illuminate not only those works but also in some degree the artistic, social and moral assumptions on which they rest. Our wish is that, in their very variety of approach and emphasis, these books will stimulate interest in and understanding of the vitality of a living literature which, because it is contemporary, is especially ours.

Norwich, England   MALCOLM BRADBURY
                                                          CHRISTOPHER BIGSBY

ACKNOWLEDGEMENTS

The author and publisher would like to thank the following for permission to reproduce copyright material: Graham Greene and William Collins Ltd for extracts from *British Dramatists*; Graham Greene and Secker & Warburg Ltd for extracts from *The Pleasure Dome*; Graham Greene, The Bodley Head, William Heinemann Ltd and Simon & Schuster, Inc. for extracts from *A Sort of Life, The Return of A. J. Raffles, The Honorary Consul, The Human Factor* and *Doctor Fischer of Geneva*; Graham Greene, The Bodley Head, William Heinemann Ltd, Simon & Schuster, Inc. and Lester & Orpen Dennys for extracts from *Ways of Escape* and *Monsignor Quixote;* Graham Greene, The Bodley Head, William Heinemann Ltd and Viking Press for extracts from *The Man Within, Stamboul Train, Brighton Rock, The Confidential Agent, The Power and the Glory, The Ministry of Fear, The Heart of the Matter, The Third Man, The End of the Affair, Loser Takes All, The Quiet American, Our Man in Havana, A Burnt-Out Case, The Comedians, Travels with my Aunt, A Sense of Reality, May We Borrow Your Husband?, Journey Without Maps, The Lawless Roads, In Search of a Character, Collected Essays, The Potting Shed* and *The Complaisant Lover*.

A NOTE ON THE TEXTS

Page references for quotations from Graham Greene's books are to the Penguin editions, unless otherwise stated. The following abbreviations have been used:

BOC	A Burnt-Out Case
BR	Brighton Rock
C	The Comedians
CA	The Confidential Agent
CE	Collected Essays
DFG	Doctor Fischer of Geneva
EA	The End of the Affair
HC	The Honorary Consul
HF	The Human Factor
HM	The Heart of the Matter
ISC	In Search of a Character
JWM	Journey Without Maps
LR	The Lawless Roads
LTA	Loser Takes All
MF	The Ministry of Fear
MW	The Man Within
MWB	May We Borrow Your Husband?
OMH	Our Man in Havana
PG	The Power and the Glory
QA	The Quiet American
SL	A Sort of Life
SR	A Sense of Reality
ST	Stamboul Train

1

PATTERNS OF MIND

'For writers it is always said that the first twenty years of life contain the whole of experience – the rest is observation, but I think it is equally true of us all' (C, p. 61). Mr Brown, owner-manager of the Hotel Trianon, Haiti, is recalling his first sexual experience in the Hôtel de Paris, Monte Carlo. He had been playing truant from his school, the Jesuit College of the Visitation, and had just won £300 in the casino when he was picked up by an older woman. Brown was at first less successful as a lover than as a gambler, until a seagull flew through the open window of the hotel room, scaring the lady and rousing the boy to play the man.

Brown's view of the importance of early experience might be considered ironic, since until his brief adventure at the casino he had been a prize pupil in Latin at his college and a promising candidate for the priesthood. Nor does anything in his youth prepare him for the events of his middle age in Haiti which he proceeds to relate in this novel, *The Comedians* (1966). By temperament and heredity an 'uncommitted' man, an observer of the violence and idealism of others, he is drawn inexorably into action on the side of the idealists. Thus his opinion seems dubious at the time he utters it, and is later shown to be false by events. Yet there is no suggestion that irony is intended. The remark is a straight *pensée* and belongs, of course, not to Brown but to Greene.

The Comedians was published in 1966. Sixteen years earlier, in an essay on 'The Young Dickens', Greene had 'inclined to believe' that 'the creative writer perceives his world once and for all in childhood and adolescence, and his whole career is an effort to illustrate his private world in terms of the great public world we all share' (*CE*, p. 83). Earlier still, in 1947, in the essay 'A Lost Childhood', he had written: 'Perhaps it is only in

11

childhood that books have any deep influence on our lives' (*CE*, p. 13), while the first sentence of his autobiography *A Sort of Life* (1971) reads: 'If I had known it, the whole future must have lain all the time along those Berkhamsted streets' (*SL*, p. 11).

Greene was born, brought up and educated in the small Hertfordshire town of Berkhamsted, where his father was headmaster of the well-known public school. The importance of that childhood and adolescence to Greene's fiction can hardly be exaggerated; but we have not quite finished with Brown. His apparently simple encounter with the older woman in Monte Carlo conceals a good deal more from the innocent first reader than Greene's obsession with childhood. There is the fact that the woman is married to a banker, conveniently absent in Saigon with a local mistress: the hero/narrator of Greene's earlier novel *The Quiet American* (1955) was a journalist living in Saigon with a Chinese mistress, while the hero/narrator of his next, *Travels with my Aunt* (1969), would be a bank manager with an adventurous, highly sexed aunt very similar to Brown's mother. Brown's parentage is vague, his father for ever unknown to him, his mother only re-encountered on her deathbed at the Hotel Trianon in the company of a young Haitian – the relationship reflecting not only Brown's with the married woman in Monte Carlo but presumably also his mother's in the same city with Brown's vanished father. The common denominator in all these associations is the contrast between a conventional and secure society (represented by bankers, Jesuit teachers and a prize pupil) and a romantic gipsy world of gambling, illicit sex and exotic travel which carries the author's seal of approval.

A further variation on the same theme is introduced by the seagull. Shortly after completing *The Quiet American*, Greene retired to Monte Carlo to gamble and to compose 'an amusing, agreeably sentimental novella' (*WE*, p. 167). Relaxing in the Hôtel de Paris after four years of reporting from the trouble-spots of the early 1950s – Malaya, Kenya, Vietnam – he wrote *Loser Takes All* (1955). The plot, partly drawn from an experience of his own with the film producer Alexander Korda, concerns a blameless assistant accountant from England and his childlike bride Cary, who find themselves stranded, by a whim of his powerful boss Dreuther – known as the Gom or Grand Old Man – in an expensive hotel in Monte Carlo. The accountant begins to gamble, perfects a winning system and is soon on the brink of being able to buy enough shares in the company he works for to revenge himself on the defaulting Gom. Unfortunately his devotion to gambling has lost him his bride to another man, and he is at his wits' end how to get her back: 'and then looking down into the harbour I saw a white boat which hadn't been there before. She was flying the British flag and I recognized her from newspaper photographs. She was the *Seagull*. The Gom had come after all' (*LTA*, p. 103). Just as 'the devil was certainly in my system', so the *Seagull*-borne Gom sets everything to rights, and the book ends happily with the accountant exchanging his devil-gotten gains for his Gom-given love.

Brown's name is even more significant than his seagull. Greene is very sparing with names. Sometimes he avoids names altogether: the hero of *The Confidential Agent* (1939) is known only as D., and the leading characters in *The Power and the Glory* (1940) only by their functions (the priest, the lieutenant, the half-caste). Sometimes he uses the same name for quite different characters in different books: there is a fat, nasty, sweet-eating Davis in *A Gun for Sale* (1936) and a perfectly nice, whisky-drinking Davis in *The Human Factor* (1978); a loud and lecherous RAF Baxter in *The Heart of the Matter* (1948) and a paper-faced commercial-travelling Baxter with heart trouble in *The Comedians*. Sometimes there seems to be a deliberate echo in the repetition: Bendrix in *The End of the Affair* (1951) and Castle in *The Human Factor* are both called Maurice, as the leading woman in both books is called Sarah. Sometimes Greene all but withholds the Christian name and then lets it out slyly so that you hardly notice it: who but the most assiduous reader remembers that Scobie in *The Heart of the Matter* is Henry or that Wormold in *Our Man in Havana* (1958) is Jim? Sometimes he never lets you know the first name at all: Brown is only Brown, as Querry in *A Burnt-Out Case* (1961) is only Querry. A little light is cast on this business of names in *The Human Factor* when the double agent Castle's black South African wife goes up to bed:

13

'Goodnight, Maurice.' The use of his name was a sign of love – when they were together it was an invitation to love. Endearments – dear and darling – were everyday currency to be employed in company, but a name was strictly private, never to be betrayed to a stranger outside the tribe. At the height of love she would cry aloud his secret tribal name. (*HF*, p. 69)

The mystery is resolved in a nightmarish story called 'Under the Garden', published in *A Sense of Reality* (1963) between *A Burnt-Out Case* and *The Comedians*, between Querry and Brown. 'Under the Garden' has an autobiographical setting, Harston House in Cambridgeshire, which belonged to Greene's uncle, Sir Graham Greene, Permanent Secretary to the Admiralty and part-model for the sympathetic and name-less Assistant Commissioner in the early novel *It's a Battlefield* (1934). As a small boy the younger Graham used to be taken to Harston for summer holidays: 'it had a large old-fashioned garden very suited to hide-and-seek, with an orchard, a stream and a big pond containing an island, and there was a fountain on the front lawn' (*SL*, p. 18). Greene borrowed this garden and especially the pond and island for the sinister clinic in his wartime novel *The Ministry of Fear* (1943), a book crucial to his 'effort to illustrate his private world in terms of the great public world we all share', an interweaving of the private theme contrasting childhood and adolescence with the public one contrasting the Victorian Pax Britannica and the European wars of the 1930s and 1940s. Not surprisingly, Brown's *pensée* pops up again here, apropos of the hero Rowe, whose 'early childhood had been passed before the First World War, and the impressions of childhood are ineffaceable' (*MF*, p. 88).

'Under the Garden' concentrates on the private theme. Its hero, William Wilditch, threatened with an operation for lung cancer (as Greene himself was in 1961), returns to the uncle's house which he had loved as a child and which is now owned by his conventional brother George. During the night William recalls the dream or actual experience – he is still not sure which – that perhaps turned him into the restless wanderer and womanizer he later became. As a boy of 7 secretly exploring the garden at night, he had crossed the pond to an island, and there

14

found an Alice-in-Wonderland tunnel leading down to a large cave under the garden. In the cave were a squalid old couple called Javitt and Maria, whose general demeanour and way of life may remind the reader partly of Samuel Beckett's Hamm and Clov in *Endgame* – Javitt is enthroned on a lavatory seat while his wife cooks him broth – but still more of the old rat and his Anna Maria in Beatrix Potter's *Samuel Whiskers*, which Greene in 1933 called her masterpiece and, with other books of her 'dark period', compared, perhaps not altogether seriously, to Henry James's mature fiction and Shakespeare's tragedies (*CE*, pp. 173–80). Javitt and Maria detain the boy Wilditch for what seems several days, while Javitt lectures him in a schoolmasterly manner on a variety of subjects. One of his topics is names, and he, or his creator, has certainly been reading T. S. Eliot's 'Naming of Cats':

> 'In the beginning you had a name only the man or woman knew who pulled you out of your mother. Then there was a name for the tribe to call you by. That was of little account, but of more account all the same than the name you had with strangers; and there was a name used in the family. . . . Up where you come from they've begun to forget the power of the name.' (*SR*, p. 44)

Broadening his theme, Javitt (not his real name) continues:

> 'Be disloyal. It's your duty to the human race. The human race needs to survive and it's the loyal man who dies first from anxiety or a bullet or overwork. If you have to earn a living, boy, and the price they make you pay is loyalty, be a double agent – and never let either of the two sides know your real name.' (*SR*, p. 48)

But the speech takes us even further into the heart of Greene's world:

> 'The same applies to women and God. They both respect a man they don't own, and they'll go on raising the price they are willing to offer. Didn't Christ say that very thing? Was the prodigal son loyal or the lost shilling or the strayed sheep? The obedient flock didn't give the shepherd any satisfaction or the loyal son interest his father.' (*SR*, p. 48)

It is the quintessential rogue's or sinner's creed which is recited, or implied, with more or less seriousness in almost every book Greene has written. Coming to the surface again, brooding over his long-ago dream or experience, the mature Wilditch anticipates Brown: 'if a child's experience does really form his future life . . .' (*SR*, p. 63).

Greene's childhood, he tells us in *A Sort of Life*, was a particularly happy one. Born in 1904, he was the fourth of six children in a large upper-middle-class Edwardian household, and, if he did not see a great deal of his parents, there were 'a nanny, a nursemaid, a gardener, a fat and cheerful cook, a beloved head-housemaid, a platoon of assistant maids, a whole battalion of aunts and uncles, all of them called Greene' (*SL*, p. 52; his mother and father were first cousins), as well as his brothers and sisters to minister to his needs. At the other end of Berkhamsted, in the big house, lived the 'rich Greenes', another branch of cousins, with six more children of roughly equivalent ages to the 'intellectual Greenes' at the School House. The settled happiness and incidental pleasures of this period when 'there was no loneliness to be experienced' echo distantly through all Greene's fiction, but especially in *The Ministry of Fear*, set mainly in London during the Blitz, when the old world seemed to be being finally, physically, expunged: 'The fête called him like innocence: it was entangled in childhood, with vicarage gardens and girls in white summer frocks and the smell of herbaceous borders and security' (*MF*, p. 11).

But this kind of security, the taken-for-granted, given kind enjoyed by a child, is not to be confused with the later kind chosen by adults, the conventional suburban life from which Aunt Augusta rescues Henry Pulling, the retired bank manager, in *Travels with my Aunt*. Cary, the young bride in *Loser Takes All*, is childlike and approved of by the author because she lives for the moment. 'In childhood,' Greene declares in *The Ministry of Fear*:

we live under the brightness of immortality – heaven is as near and actual as the seaside. Behind the complicated details of the world stand the simplicities: God is good, the grown-up man or woman knows the answer to every question, there is such a thing as truth, and justice is as measured and faultless as a clock. Our heroes are simple: they are brave, they tell the truth, they are good swordsmen and they are never in the long run really defeated. That is why no later books satisfy us like those which were read to us in childhood – for those promised a world of great simplicity of which we knew the rules, but the later books are complicated and contradictory with experience. (*MF*, pp. 88–9)

Childhood in Greene's world is the nearest thing to heaven on earth: a time of peace, trust, confident identity, relaxed communal living, absence of those twin anxieties loss and hope and, above all, through the medium of children's fiction, of magically reconciling perfect taken-for-granted security with unlimited adventure. If his own fiction often seems desolate and pessimistic, it is not because it contains no glimpses of a better world; on the contrary, like the blue passages that aerate Cézanne's landscapes, this better world is constantly flashing its signals to us:

'Don't worry,' like a whisper lodged in the ear, a summer sound belonging to childhood. (*EA*, p. 137)

'To start off happy,' Harris said. 'It must make an awful difference afterwards. Why, it might become a habit, mightn't it?' (*HM*, p. 140)

Happiness is a habit for Mr Smith, the childlike vegetarian and former US presidential candidate in *The Comedians*: 'He had been born with peace in his heart instead of the splinter of ice' (*C*, p. 246). Greene's two most vicious protagonists, Raven in *A Gun for Sale* and Pinkie in *Brighton Rock* (1938), both deprived of happiness in childhood, are both described as having splinters of ice in their hearts. Recalling an occasion when he himself had been in hospital and coldly observed the reactions of the parents of a child who had just died, Greene remarks in *A Sort of Life* that 'there is a splinter of ice in the heart of a writer' (*SL*, p. 134). Most of Greene's protagonists, though, live between the habit and the splinter of ice: happiness is a memory or dream of something for ever out of reach in the past.

17

Greene's expulsion from Eden came in his thirteenth year, when he entered the senior part of his father's school. He had joined the junior school at the age of 8, but apparently 'the clouds of unknowing were still luminous with happiness' (*SL*, p. 52), and, in spite of the outbreak of the First World War when he was 10, the pleasant routines of his family life – interspersed with the safe adventures provided by Henty and Haggard, Westerman, Weyman and Stevenson – continued as before. Greene's unhappiness in the senior school was caused not by physical bullying but by the fact that he was now boarding – with all the prison-like accompaniments of loneliness, squalor and loss of identity which that entailed in an English public school, even one with a relatively liberal headmaster who was his own father; that, indeed, was the worst element in Greene's agony, his conflicting loyalties. A boy called Carter, he says, 'perfected during my fourteenth and fifteenth years a system of mental torture based on my difficult situation' and another boy called Watson, previously Greene's friend, 'deserted me for Carter' (*SL*, p. 60). Carter's name crops up again in *Our Man in Havana*: he is the villain, at first sly and murderous, eventually pathetic and murdered. Watson's name is borrowed for the heroine of the short story, 'Cheap in August', who deceives her husband with an elderly American remittance-man in the Caribbean but seems too sympathetically treated to have much connection with the original Watson. Perhaps he is transmuted into the would-be poet and overgrown schoolboy Wilson, who spies on and cuckolds Major Scobie in *The Heart of the Matter*.

At any rate, in Greene's fiction, adolescence is to childhood as hell is to heaven. He himself, homesick (though his home was so near), mistrustful, betrayed, excluded, tormented, first took to truancy, then to attempts at suicide and at last to running away. A course of psychoanalysis in London returned him to school with much-needed cachet and a new self-confidence, but the horrible three-year experience of life in a world of strangers and enemies remained for ever central to his imagination. Whatever the nominal age of his central characters in his books, they are, most of them, still trapped within adolescence and its immediate aftermath; they have never discovered a satisfying way out into adult life. The choice –

which is not, of course, a true one, since Greene is interested only in the second alternative – lies between the cul-de-sac of a lifeless suburban respectability and the marginally greater freedom of being a nomad – unattached, insecure, disloyal, sometimes hunted and threatened, but alive and preferably living under an assumed or partly concealed name. As the reformed bank manager Henry Pulling puts it in *Travels with my Aunt*:

> I was afraid of burglars and Indian thugs and snakes and fires and Jack the Ripper, when I should have been afraid of thirty years in a bank and a take-over bid and a premature retirement and the Deuil du Roy Albert [one of the dahlias he grows in his garden]. (*TA*, p. 163)

Just as there is in practice only one choice, so there is really only one protagonist. In 1934, after leaving Oxford, working as a journalist for *The Nottingham Journal* and *The Times*, and publishing his first five novels, Greene persuaded one of the 'rich Greenes', his cousin Barbara, to accompany him on a trek through Liberia. There, as he records in *Journey Without Maps* (1936), quite soon after crossing the border from Sierra Leone, they witnessed a dance by Landow, the local 'devil' or priest:

> A masked devil like Landow . . . might roughly be described as a headmaster with rather more supernatural authority than Arnold of Rugby ever claimed. . . . most natives, if they are not Mohammedan, will attend a bush school, of which the masked devil is the unknown head. . . . And the bush schools are very secret. . . . The school and the devil who rules over it are at first a terror to the child. It lies as grimly as a public school in England between childhood and manhood. . . . no human part of the devil is allowed to show. . . . Even though the initiates of his particular school, who have seen, as it were, the devil in his off-moments, know him to be, say, the local blacksmith, some supernatural feeling continues to surround him. It is not the mask which is sacred, nor the blacksmith who is sacred; it is the two in conjunction. (*JWM*, pp. 89–90)

Greene's relationship to his central characters is almost exactly that of this Liberian blacksmith to his costume: they are the wooden snouted mask, the headdress of feathers, the heavy blanket robe and the long raffia mane and skirts; he is the controlling inhabitant, headmasterly too in his pronouncements and improving *pensées*, a devil, priest or Javitt come to judgement and instruction on the secrets of growing up, but also a dancer and entertainer:

> The spirit was definitely carnival. . . . but it wasn't a carnival in the vulgar sense of Nice and the Battle of Flowers; it wasn't secular and skittish; like the dancing in the Spanish cathedral at Easter, it had its religious value. (*JWM*, p. 92)

Greene had gone to Liberia in search of the primitive: 'my journey represented a distrust of any future based on what we are' (*JWM*, p. 20). He was looking for the racial past, 'the primal memory', the childhood of humanity as a whole, but Africa also meant for him, of course, *King Solomon's Mines*, *Prester John* and *The Heart of Darkness*: 'we were a generation brought up on adventure stories who had missed the enormous disillusionment of the First World War, so we went looking for adventure' (*WE*, p. 37). Even eight years later, sailing out in convoy to his wartime Secret Service assignment in Freetown, he noted, repeating an image he had first used in his account of the Liberian expedition, that 'Africa will always be the Africa of the Victorian atlas, the blank unexplored continent the shape of the human heart' (*ISC*, p. 105).

He found what he was looking for, 'the moments of extra-ordinary happiness' and 'the instinctive way of life'. But on this long, exhausting tramp through the bush he recovered

> the boredom of childhood too, that agonizing boredom of 'apartness' which came before one had learnt the fatal trick of transferring emotion, of flashing back enchantingly all day long one's own image, a period when other people were as distinct from oneself as this Liberian forest. I sometimes wonder whether, if one had stayed longer, if one had not been driven out again by tiredness and fear, one might have relearned the way to live without transference, with a lost objectivity. (*JWM*, p. 158)

An odd passage, an odd jumble of notions. 'Apartness' is boring, but it is a 'trick', even a fatal one, to 'transfer emotion'.

Does he mean that it's fatal to love other people or that it's fatal to think you are loving them when in reality you are using them only as a mirror for your self-love? The last sentence of the quotation suggests that it would be better if love didn't come into it at all, that one might learn to grow up away from love, even presumably at the price of boredom. The 'devil's' dance which Greene performs inside the masks and costumes of his protagonists is much concerned with this knotty theme: love, lust, self-sufficiency. It is clearly the trickiest part of the syllabus in his bush school for those between childhood and manhood, and he never satisfactorily resolves it.

WOMEN AND MEN

Before setting out for Liberia, Barbara Greene took stock of her cousin, whom she hadn't previously had much to do with. 'Always remember to rely on yourself,' she wrote in her diary. 'If you are in a sticky place he will be so interested in noting your reactions that he will probably forget to rescue you.'[1] She had already noticed the splinter of ice. As it turned out, he came nearer to dying (of fever) than she did, but their relationship, according to both their published accounts, seems to have remained a distant one. She, near the rear of the column (walking more often than not, according to her account, but according to his being carried in a hammock), became increasingly irritated by the sight of him striding away at the head of the column with his socks falling down. He, on the other hand, resented her shorts, voluminous but very brief. When they were together over meals in their halting-places, they studiously avoided all subjects likely to be controversial and were reduced eventually to the single topic of food. Far from noting her reactions, Greene almost excludes her from his book; one is conscious of her only as a kind of ghost in abominable shorts somewhere at the back of the column. Greene is extremely reticent about his private life in his autobiographical writings, and we should not read too much into one experience; nevertheless, the leading ladies of his fiction are, almost without exception, ghosts too. They can be crudely categorized, according to the period of the novels, into *princesses lointaines* alternating with vulnerable, subservient shop- or

21

chorus-girls (pre-war); tenderly adoring mistresses, usually married to conventional but complaisant husbands (post-war); and, in the last two novels, flawless young wives. The exceptions are Scobie's wife Louise in *The Heart of the Matter* and Aunt Augusta in *Travels with my Aunt*, the former a living and touching portrait of an unhappy woman, the latter more a Shavian Life Force – a female version of Javitt – than a person, but at least self-propelled. The rest of the leading ladies seem to be wheeled on and off only to perform the office of flashing back the image of the protagonist.

There is nothing surprising in this: much as he admires Henry James, Greene's own fiction is firmly in the tradition of the male adventure story. Does one remember Dickens's heroines, Stevenson's, Conrad's, except as mirrors to the protagonists? Even less so the heroines of Greene's favourite second-league writers – Haggard, Westerman, Weyman, Buchan. Henry Pulling, the loveless bank manager, muses:

> One's life is more formed, I sometimes think, by books than by human beings; it is out of books one learns about love and pain at second hand. Even if we have the happy chance to fall in love, it is because we have been conditioned by what we have read, and if I had never known love at all, perhaps it was because my father's library had not contained the right books. (*TA*, p. 203)

The heroine of Greene's first published novel, *The Man Within* (1929), is a purely romantic *princesse lointaine*, and the author makes his apologies for her unreality through the mouth of his protagonist: 'You'll never find a man who will love you for anything but a bare, unfilled-in outline of yourself. . . . Only a woman can love a real person' (*MW*, p. 65). In the anti-romantic novels of the 1930s, love is seen chiefly as an instrument of exploitation and betrayal, and there is a powerful undertow of disgust for the sexual act, especially in *Brighton Rock* (1938). Pinkie, the teenage murderer whose childhood hell partly consisted of 'the frightening weekly exercise of his parents which he watched from his single bed', marries Rose to prevent her giving evidence against him, but then finds himself confronted with 'the last human shame':

That was what they expected of you, every polony you met had her eye on the bed; his virginity straightened in him like sex. That was how they judged you; not by whether you had the guts to kill a man, to run a mob. (*BR*, p. 91)

Pinkie, of course, is a special case, Greene's attempt to inhabit the most vicious and frightening mask he could imagine, red-toothed adolescence with hardly a dab of childhood blue to soften it, a slum Carter with no holds barred. None the less, travelling in Mexico that same year (1938) and observing in a little square in Monterrey 'demure courtships going on upon every bench', Greene echoes Pinkie's sentiments:

It was as if these people hadn't the need for lechery. . . . They didn't feel the need of proving their manhood by pressing on the deed of darkness before its time. Fear was eliminated: they each knew where the other stood. One was not thinking, 'What does she expect me to do?' nor the other, 'How far can I let him go?' They were happy together in the dark bound by the rules of a game they both knew; no fear, no exasperated nerves. (*LR*, pp. 31–2)

He admits he was taking 'the tourist view', but 'the deed of darkness' is rather over-emphatic and his comparison with London even more so: 'I thought of the couples sprawling in ugly passion on the Hyde Park grass or on chairs performing uglier acts under the shelter of overcoats.'

The sense of sexual disgust is still apparent in *The Power and the Glory* (1940), expressed particularly through the character of the despicable Padre José, a priest who has accepted marriage to 'an enormous shape in a white nightshirt' in preference to execution by the anticlerical authorities. But a new idea has crept into the book: 'Lust', the good priest wants to tell one of those confessing to him, 'is not the worst thing. It is because any day, any time, lust may turn into love that we have to avoid it' (*PG*, p. 172). The explanation for this paradox given by the priest is a conventionally religious one: 'when we love our sin then we are damned indeed'. But in *The Ministry of Fear* and even more *The Heart of the Matter* (1948) the idea grows into a major theme. 'Was it the butterfly that died in the act of love,' wonders Scobie, after he has slept with his mistress for the first time. 'But human beings were condemned to consequences. The responsibility as well as the guilt was his' (*HM*, p. 154). Love now is recognized as pity – 'the terrible promiscuous passion which so few experience' – and the dangerous qualities in a person of the other sex are failure, ugliness and pathos, not beauty, grace or intelligence. Greene seems to have meant his readers to see Scobie's pity as only an emanation of pride and self-love, but in his next book, *The End of the Affair* (1951), he purges the theme of its selfish element by pursuing it through Sarah, the saintly leading lady, who, in a plot reminiscent of Euripides' play *Alcestis*, sacrifices herself to save her lover. It is really only what Scobie does, but Sarah is after all a woman and Greene is as courtly towards his leading ladies as he is hard on his male protagonists. In other words, he takes the latter more seriously: the main theme of *The End of the Affair* is the protagonist Bendrix's furiously possessive love, which turns to jealousy and hatred when the possession is removed.

Just as the original blacksmith-devil in Liberia went on too long with his dance, so in the novels written during the 1950s Greene's devil-dance of one-sided love becomes increasingly mechanical. There is more than a hint of the TV commercial about this exchange in his second play, *The Potting Shed* (1958):

> JAMES. My father's dying. . . . When he looks at me, don't you think I might see – just love? No claim, no hope, no want. Whiskey taken neat.
> SARA. The strong taste.[2]

A Burnt-Out Case (1961) is as much as anything an acceptance that this is a burnt-out theme: 'never again', promises Querry, 'from boredom or vanity to involve another human being in my lack of love' (*BOC*, p. 118).

Of course, characters continue to love one another sexually in Greene's later work, but the subject is no longer treated as a personal challenge, a psychological and even metaphysical conundrum, a spiritual ordeal. The narrator of the title story in *May We Borrow Your Husband?* (1967), who hardly troubles to wear much of a mask over the Greene inside, is ready to explain to a young, unhappy bride that

'... the only love which has lasted is the love that has accepted everything, every disappointment, every failure and every betrayal, which has accepted even the sad fact that in the end there is no desire so deep as the simple desire for companionship.' (*MWB*, pp. 27–8)

Brown in *The Comedians* reckons that he and his leading lady found their happiest moment talking rather than making love. Dr Plarr, the philandering protagonist of *The Honorary Consul* (1973), seems momentarily to revive the old conundrum when he distinguishes 'the sickness' of 'I love' from the other 'maladies' such as loneliness, pride, physical desire or curiosity (for Pinkie it was sexual desire that was 'like a sickness'); but it is the honorary consul Charlie Fortnum's simple companionship with his passive ex-prostitute wife Clara that emerges victorious.

In two recent novels, Greene raises this idea of companionship to a new status: the domestic security of a successful marriage becomes the substitute for childhood's taken-for-granted security and as such the centre of the action. For like childhood it can be threatened by the adolescent forces of violence, imprisonment and exile: 'A man in love', thinks Castle, protagonist of *The Human Factor* (1978), 'walks through the world like an anarchist, carrying a time bomb' (*HF*, p. 141). Like childhood it can be removed altogether, sealed off in the past: Jones, the narrator of *Doctor Fischer of Geneva* (1980), whose fairy-tale wife dies in a skiing accident, says, 'Love ceases to be happiness. Love becomes a sense of intolerable loss' (*DFG*, p. 64).

BIG TERMS

There is a curious similarity between this Greene, with his unreal women in squalid circumstances, and an earlier one – Robert Greene, the Elizabethan playwright who called Shakespeare 'an upstart crow', and of whom Graham Greene wrote: 'Greene with his idealized milkmaids, cool-fingered, spiritual and content, who ranged the air above the dreary room, the alehouse and the stews which formed his actual scene'.[3] Graham Greene was finishing *British Dramatists*

(1942), his contribution to a series called 'Britain in Pictures', on his way out to West Africa in 1941. Later he wondered 'was it the rough seas and cold watches that made me write so harshly of Congreve?' (*ISC*, p. 98). Surely not. It was that Congreve, more than any other British playwright except Shakespeare (and Greene's attention was focused on other facets of Shakespeare's genius), understood love as a two-sided, realistic relationship and could show both sides of it with the same sympathy and objectivity. Congreve's characters were simply too worldly for Greene's taste; they had too much of the 'flesh' and not enough of the 'religious sense'.

Greene reads the history of British drama in a special way. The greatness of Shakespeare is that 'here is the watershed between the morality and the play of character',[4] since the morality play is 'the bones without the flesh' and 'in twentieth century drama we have the flesh without the bones – characters who act a plot before us and have no significance at all outside the theatre'.[5] The 'bones', the significance Greene admires, is an abstraction; it is the theme or 'attitude to life' for which the characters are mouthpieces. In Shakespeare, so close still to the morality play, 'the abstraction – the spirit of Revenge (Hamlet), of Jealousy (Othello), of Ambition (Macbeth), of Ingratitude (Lear), of Passion (Antony and Cleopatra) – still rules the play.'[6] And further on he adds that 'the old abstract drama had dealt with important things: with "the base Indian who threw a pearl away richer than all his tribe", with the lark in the cage and the soul in the body.' Alas, a century and a half after Shakespeare,

> that had gone, perhaps for ever, and the theatre had become a kind of supplement to *The Ladies' Magazine*. The religious sense was at its lowest ebb, and the political did not exist as we know it today. Man's interests shrank like a rockpool in the hard bright sunlight of reason.[7]

The passage is a digest of Greene's theory and practice as a novelist. Four years later, in 1945, he extended his judgement on post-Restoration drama to the post-Jamesian novel:

> with the death of James the religious sense was lost to the English novel, and with the religious sense went the sense of the importance of the human act. It was as if the world

of fiction had lost a dimension: the characters of such distinguished writers as Mrs Virginia Woolf and Mr E. M. Forster wandered like cardboard symbols through a world that was paper-thin. (*CE*, p. 91)

Except that James ('he is as solitary in the history of the novel', he had written in 1936, 'as Shakespeare in the history of poetry'; *CE*, p. 34) stands in for Shakespeare, and Woolf and Forster for *The Ladies' Magazine*, the two passages are almost identical. Greene saw his own task as a novelist very specifically as the retrieval of that 'lost dimension', which is the other world of the morality plays and Christian teaching, the grand backdrop of the struggle between good and evil, the 'religious sense'. He wanted this dimension in his novels not so much because he was converted to Catholicism at the age of 22 as for literary and temperamental reasons: without it the fictional stakes were not high enough, the action not important or significant enough; furthermore, in any contest in which mere rationality and mundane realism held the ring it was certain that suburban security – the bankers, the prize pupils and *The Ladies' Magazine* – would come out on top.

As I have already suggested, one has to distinguish in Greene's fiction between the two sorts of security: on the one hand, the dreary, conventional, chosen one – symbolized in *A Sort of Life* by the commuters of Berkhamsted and their anonymous houses – and, on the other, the given, magical one of childhood – symbolized by the historical and Greene-inhabited parts of Berkhamsted. So too one has to distinguish between two sorts of abstractions: those that belong to the grand world of good and evil and those that belong to the petty humanistic world of right and wrong. The distinction is hammered home in *Brighton Rock*, in the contrast between Pinkie, the sexually repressed, damned soul, and Ida Arnold, the suburban and sexually easygoing barmaid who takes it upon herself to hunt him down. But unless one is well acquainted with Greene's work it can be confusing. He admires Shakespeare and the morality plays because they give primacy to the spirit of Revenge, Jealousy, Ambition, etc., but there are frequent slighting references in his work to what Brown in *The Comedians* calls 'the big terms I could not recognize, like Mankind, Justice, the Pursuit of Happiness'

27

(*C*, p. 113). There seem to be good 'big terms' and bad 'big terms'.

The distinction is somewhat clarified in Greene's travel book about Mexico, *The Lawless Roads* (1939), where he takes a dislike to Rivera's painting of 'The Son' in his fresco *Creation*: 'what is he but Progress, Human Dignity, great empty Victorian conceptions that life denies at every turn?' (*L R*, p.70). And he goes on to compare Rivera to two High Victorian painters, Leighton and Watts. So, although for Greene (especially in *The Ministry of Fear*) the Victorian age sometimes stands for peace and childhood as against the violence and adolescence of the mid-twentieth century, it also stands for bogus and grandiose ideas. This double view extends to Greene's childhood reading: it is both good because it offers adventure and bad because its heroes are 'of such unyielding integrity (they would only admit to a fault in order to show how it might be overcome). . . . These men were like Platonic ideas: they were not life as one had already begun to know it' (*CE*, p. 16).

His first way out of this difficulty was literary, his second religious. When he was about 14 he read Marjorie Bowen's historical romance of Renaissance Italy called *The Viper of Milan* (1906). The difference between this and all his previous romantic reading was that not only did it end disastrously for all the characters but even the hero behaved badly and betrayed his friends. As for the villain 'Visconti, with his beauty, his patience, and his genius for evil, I had watched him pass by many a time in his black Sunday suit smelling of mothballs. His name was Carter' (*CE*, pp. 16–17). So literature at last caught up with Greene's experience of adolescent reality and he saw that it was possible to extract romance and adventure from the unheroic, the disloyal, the weak, the failed, the post-Victorian. In the process of adapting this discovery to his own needs he also to some extent re-identified the villain. It was not so much Visconti/Carter, the incarnation of evil – whom he rather admired and who, in his various reincarnations in Greene's work, is nearer to being a hero – as a mainly faceless politburo of the smug, the invulnerable, the successful. The big terms expressing their cold virtues were bad, whereas the big terms expressing the warm emotions – Revenge, Jealousy, Passion, etc. – of a fallible post-Victorian anti-hero were good. Beyond

28

Carter, after all, was the original cause of Greene's misery: his parents (above all his father), their self-confidently imperial generation, their educational system and all the hinterland of established British values.

It was only to be expected, then, that, aged 19, while he was still at Oxford, he should have briefly joined the Communist Party (briefly, because its materialism went entirely against his grain); and that having left Oxford in 1925 he should have taken a job on a local paper in Nottingham, a place he would afterwards look back on with the same affection reserved for Berkhamsted and West Africa. Nottingham represented his first independent choice of a fresh background, 'the focal point of failure, a place undisturbed by ambition, a place to be resigned to, a home from home' (*SL*, p. 115). He was remaking his life from the beginning according to his improved view of reality. The unexpected thing was that, while in Nottingham, he should have become a Roman Catholic. True, he was about to marry a Roman Catholic, and it may have been another form of revolt against his conventional, middle-class, Anglican background; but Roman Catholicism was surely a paternalistic establishment still more rigid than the one he had rejected. Perhaps that was part of its attraction. Greene, it must be clear by now, thrives on emotional contradictions. At any rate, it offered him as a writer the grand cosmic backdrop he wanted, the religious sense which would supply ulterior significance and importance to the obscure lives of futility and defeat that he insisted on for his post-Victorian characters.

THE LOST DIMENSION

He did not at first make much fictional use of his new faith. The lonely heroine of his first published novel, *The Man Within* (1929), is supported by her religion, but its nature is left vague. This and the next two novels were essentially historical romances, deriving distantly from Marjorie Bowen and Anthony Hope and more closely from Conrad. *The Man Within* was a considerable commercial success, selling more than 8000 copies. The comparative failure of *The Name of Action* (1930) and *Rumour at Nightfall* (1931) pushed the now rather desperate Greene, who had thrown up his job with *The Times* to become a professional novelist, into a new genre, the thriller with a modern and realistic setting. Conrad (especially his *The Secret Agent*) was still an influence, but so was Buchan:

> John Buchan was the first to realize the enormous dramatic value of adventure in familiar surroundings happening to unadventurous men, members of Parliament and members of the Athenaeum, lawyers and barristers, business men and minor peers: murder in 'the atmosphere of breeding and simplicity and stability'. Richard Hannay, Sir Edward Leithen, Mr Blenkiron, Archie Roylance, and Lord Lamancha; these were his adventurers, not Dr Nikola or the Master of Ballantrae, and who will forget the first thrill in 1916 as the hunted Leithen − the future Solicitor-General − ran 'like a thief in a London thoroughfare on a June afternoon'? (*CE*, p. 167)

Greene admired 'the completeness of the world' described by Buchan, but of course it was the wrong world, that of the old Victorian establishment, its ideals false, its treasure banked in worldly success. His own political thrillers of the 1930s, some of which he termed 'entertainments', aimed for Buchan's completeness and familiar ordinariness without his system of values. The only values left in these books are the vulnerable innocence of childhood; a vague desire to help the underdog and improve the lot of mankind (the characters moved by this desire, such as Czinner in *Stamboul Train* and D. in *The Confidential Agent*, are political idealists of almost ludicrous impracticality and passivity); and a certain dogged sense of public responsibility in policemen such as the Assistant Commissioner in *It's a Battlefield* and Mather in *A Gun for Sale*. A battlefield it is, a hopeless, broken-winged world, Jacobean in its gloom, Jacobean too in the energetic relish of the storyteller; in *British Dramatists* Greene, predictably, admired Webster and remarked that he excelled Shakespeare in his expression of 'the night side of life'.

The violent actions of these thrillers, the races between hunters and hunted to a climax, and the techniques of swift cutting and vivid camera-like observation, remind one that Greene was a film critic for four years in the late 1930s. But particularly in *It's a Battlefield* and the short story 'The Basement Room' (1935; filmed under the title *The Fallen Idol*, 1948), which are set in London, and in the London scenes of *England Made Me* (1935), *A Gun for Sale* and *The Confidential Agent*, one is conscious, under the carefully researched realism, of a fascinated distaste for the urban desolation of dust, refuse, smoke and zombie-like strangers. This is as much the 'unreal City' of T. S. Eliot's *The Waste Land* as it is the real London. Even in *Stamboul Train*, which begins on the other side of the Channel, Myatt the Jewish merchant from London has 'a pocket full of currants' just like Eliot's 'Mr Eugenides, the Smyrna merchant'.[8]

Greene tells us that 'T. S. Eliot and Herbert Read were the two great figures of my young manhood' (*WE*, p. 33), and in an essay written in 1933 he quotes Eliot on Baudelaire: 'It is true to say that the glory of man is his capacity for salvation; it is also true to say that his glory is his capacity for damnation' (*CE*, p. 41). The word 'glory' crops up again in Greene's assessment of Read, whose 'ruling passion' as a writer was 'the search for glory'. Read wished to dissociate 'glory' from its discredited public meanings – military grandeur, fame and ambition. Greene quotes him in *Ways of Escape* (1980):

'True glory is a private and discreet virtue, and is only fully realized in solitariness.' . . . 'At certain moments the individual is carried beyond his rational self, on to another ethical plane, where his actions are judged by new standards. The impulse which moves him to irrational action I have called the sense of glory.' (*WE*, pp. 35–6)

Eliot's Christian notion of glory – the capacity for salvation or damnation – and Read's secular notion of glory – a kind of secret heroism – underlie, separately or in combination, most of Greene's mature fiction.

However, with *Brighton Rock* (1938), Greene's new faith at last emerged in his fiction. The novel started as another 'entertainment', a thriller set in Brighton among the racecourse gangs; and its teenage hero, Pinkie, was to have been a further version of Raven in *A Gun for Sale*, a second killer with a ruined childhood and a splinter of ice in his heart (Raven, indeed, was the man who killed Pinkie's predecessor as gang leader). Greene was obviously still trying to create a contem-

31

porary equivalent to Visconti, the Viper of Milan. In 1937, reviewing the film of Maxwell Anderson's *Winterset*, he warmed particularly to a killer called Trock: 'In this character, acted with evil magnificence by Eduardo Ciannelli, there is some of the poetry of a Renaissance tyrant, with basilisks in the eyes and the everlasting cold pinching the heart.'[9] But Pinkie swelled to grander proportions. He turned out to be not just another criminal in a bad world but one, born a Catholic, who believed in his own damnation and gloried in it: 'he trailed the clouds of his own glory after him: hell lay about him in his infancy. He was ready for more deaths' (*BR*, p. 69). In this novel, for the first time Greene recovers his 'lost dimension', the 'religious sense' which had gone out with Henry James. Like Faust and Don Juan, Pinkie disappears into the abyss at the end, even if it is only off a Sussex cliff, his face burning from his own phial of vitriol: 'it was as if he'd been withdrawn suddenly by a hand out of any existence – past or present, whipped away into zero – nothing' (*BR*, p. 245).

Powerful and disturbing though it is in patches, *Brighton Rock* turns mawkish and melodramatic with the coming together of its villain/hero and his impossibly sanctified heroine. But for Greene it was clearly a kind of lift-off. He could have his futile, fallen, existential world and his glory too. His own belief in Catholicism was not really the point; so long as his characters believed, they could act as lightning-conductors for the cosmic struggle of good and evil. Here, after all, right under his nose, was exactly the system of values that corresponded to his needs: older and more authoritative than Buchan's or his parents', yet also, in England at least, associated with outlawry and a persecuted minority; colourful as well as inexorable in its rewards and punishments; paradoxical in its special care for the sinner and the failure; beyond rational human understanding in its one-sided, all-embracing love. And it was full of secrets: the secrets of the confessional, the secret presence of God in the world, the secret glory of unrecognized saints and, above all, the possibility of a secret mercy towards sinners even when the seemingly unforgivable sin had been committed. Spies, double agents, betrayers, suicides, murderers: all might be secretly justified when infinite love rather than human reason was the judge.

Writing *Brighton Rock* and glimpsing all these riches must have been as exciting as finding a box of treasure buried in one's own garden – as Wilditch does, led by Javitt, in 'Under the Garden'. Greene still considers that *Brighton Rock* is perhaps 'one of the best I ever wrote' and recalls that the characters seemed to transform the real Brighton he knew into an imaginary city: 'I have never again felt so much the victim of my own inventions' (*WE*, p. 62). It is another way of saying that his imagination was released and had found the way it wanted to go.

Since his conversion in 1926, Greene's Catholicism had been of a fairly formal kind – he went regularly to church and confession and he read a good deal of theology: 'I had not been emotionally moved, but only intellectually convinced' (*WE*, p. 58). Now, in 1937, just as the faith was coming alive for him in his fiction, it was also coming alive in the contemporary world. In Spain the Catholics were fighting against Franco, and in Mexico the socialist authorities were persecuting Catholics in the provinces of Tabasco and Chiapas. Greene used the Spanish struggle – its political rather than its religious aspect – for another 'entertainment', *The Confidential Agent* (1939), a book he wrote at great speed 'with the automatism of a planchette' for money (*WE*, p. 69). Chronologically it comes after *Brighton Rock*, but it belongs to the pre-*Brighton Rock* group of thrillers, with their background of European violence and their weary wasteland atmosphere unrelieved by any 'religious sense'. It was Mexico which confirmed the promise of *Brighton Rock*, and which set him on course through his series of four more 'Catholic' novels; also eventually through the series of post-war 'political' novels from *The Quiet American* to *The Human Factor*, whose background is Third World violence and whose protagonists are solitary, uncommitted men, aspiring to Read's sober, stoic glory rather than Eliot's flamboyant, metaphysical kind.

2

CATHOLIC NOVELS

Greene first tried to get into Spain and failed. However, he was commissioned to write a book about the religious persecution in Mexico and spent the spring of 1938 there. The immediate results were a travel book, *The Lawless Roads* (1939), and a novel, *The Power and the Glory* (1940). The two are very closely related. Greene's Liberian experiences of 1934, diffused into later experiences of Sierra Leone and the Congo, were not drawn upon in his fiction until many years afterwards. But *The Power and the Glory* contains scenes, characters and observations lifted directly from *The Lawless Roads*. If *Brighton Rock* was set partly in a city of the mind, a suburb of hell which bore superficial resemblances to the real Brighton, *The Power and the Glory* is sharply authentic, shot as it were on location in hell itself, with most of the parts played by genuine locals. Greene did not meet the original of the protagonist but heard his story and conflated it to some extent with that of Father Damien, a priest and perhaps saint in a leper colony in the Pacific who had been attacked by a Protestant pastor for his 'vices and negligence' and defended by R. L. Stevenson. Damien had been one of the heroes of Greene's childhood reading, and he even considered writing his biography.

Pinkie's attempt to impose his adolescent rule on Brighton was a dismal failure, but pre-war Mexico, as Greene saw it in *The Lawless Roads*, was a place given up to adolescents:

> It is this boyishness, this immaturity, which gets most on the nerves in Mexico. Grown men cannot meet in the street without sparring like schoolboys. One must be as a little child, we are told, to enter the kingdom of heaven, but they have passed childhood and remain for ever in a cruel anarchic adolescence. (*LR*, p. 69)

A subject peculiarly suited to his hand. *The Lawless Roads* begins with a reminiscence of himself as a 13-year-old on his father's dark croquet-lawn – just on the right side of the border between his beloved home and his hated school, which were separated indoors only by the green baize door near his father's study. The theme of *Journey Without Maps* was the search for a primeval childhood; that of *The Lawless Roads* is crossing the border into adolescence. Mexico, of course, is not as bad as Berkhamsted School, if only because Greene is now a tourist, a visiting Dante, rather than an inmate of the Inferno. Moreover, the Mexican horror is alleviated by the Catholic faith of the ordinary inhabitants, even though that is also the cause of their persecution: 'Here were idolatry and oppression, starvation and casual violence, but you lived under the shadow of religion – of God or the Devil' (*LR*, p. 184).

There is a curious discrepancy between Greene's account of his schooldays in *A Sort of Life* and the reminiscence at the beginning of *The Lawless Roads*, written some thirty-two years earlier. Recounting in the former how he first took Catholic instruction out of interest in his Catholic fiancée's theology, he remarks that 'to me religion went no deeper than the sentimental hymns in the school chapel' (*SL*, p. 118). Yet alone on the croquet-lawn, on the peaceful side of the border, the school orchestra playing Mendelssohn in the distance, he describes in *The Lawless Roads* how

> One became aware of God with an intensity – time hung suspended – music lay on the air; anything might happen before it became necessary to join the crowd across the border . . . faith was almost great enough to move mountains. . . . And so faith came to one – shapelessly, without dogma, a presence above a croquet lawn, something associated with violence, cruelty, evil across the way. One began to believe in heaven because one believed in hell. (*LR*, p. 14)

It sounds like a true experience, but perhaps it was after all only a backward leap of the imagination, now, in 1938, fully stirred by the romance of faith. At any rate, much of the power of *The Power and the Glory* derives from Greene's intense identification with the protagonist, the unnamed whisky priest who alone defies the authorities and keeps faith alive in his corner of

35

hell. His author could imagine exactly what it was like, deliberately to return across the border from peace, safety and a sense of personal dignity into fear, degradation and death by firing-squad. He could even imagine that one did it to music – the priest starts to whistle a tune as he follows his half-caste Judas back into the hands of the authorities. But faith he could locate only as a sense of duty – the priest is lured back to hear a dying man's confession, though he knows it is an ambush – for in Greene's own adolescent experience 'it was only hell one could picture with a certain intimacy' and 'the Anglican Church could not supply the same intimate symbols for heaven' (*LR*, p. 14).

Ten years after it was published, *The Power and the Glory* was condemned by the Holy Office for being 'paradoxical' and for dealing 'with extraordinary circumstances'. For them, presumably, the faith did not shine brightly enough out of the surrounding gloom; but for non-Catholic readers it is precisely the personal, dogged, earth-bound nature of the priest's faith, the fact that the religious sense is not objectified in anything so out-of-the-way as even 'a presence above a croquet lawn', which makes the book credible and sympathetic. Yet the grander faith is there; not in the priest on the ground, as it were, but in the romantic nature of the book. For, although the squalid life and death of this trembling, alcoholic martyr is ironically contrasted in the novel with the life of another more conventional martyr as related in a typical piece of pious Catholic propaganda, it *is* a story of heroism and it *is* a story of the Catholic faith being stronger and better than its persecutors.

Richard Hoggart, in an essay called 'The Force of Caricature', has dissected 'the skilled over-forcing of style, structure and character' and 'the impression of management from outside' in this novel, and his analysis of Greene's rhetorical distortion, his 'immense readability', applies more or less to all his work. Hoggart goes on to say that he is not accusing Greene of aiming at commercial success, and that 'it seems more likely that both the distortion and the excessive control are results of Greene's view of life'.[10] Of course. The 'view of life' is the persistent survival in Greene of the atmosphere of his childhood reading, the continuing search for 'the high romantic tale', as he calls it in *Ways of Escape*, which at this stage in his career he had identified as 'the religious sense' and squared for the moment with the teaching, if not always the practice, of the Roman Catholic Church. The view of life rules this book, as it rules others, and distorts, for instance, the character of the priest's socialist opponent, the lieutenant of police, presenting him as little more than an abstraction in a morality play; it does not rule, so much as emanate from, the priest, reliving Greene's own adolescence with hardly an inkling of 'glory', 'faith' or any mitigation whatever.

There is the same division between the highly 'managed' novel and the almost free character at its centre in Greene's next Catholic novel, *The Heart of the Matter* (1948). Its setting and much of its detail are based on Greene's stint with the Secret Service in Sierra Leone during the Second World War. Major Scobie, the protagonist, deputy commissioner of police in the colony, is that rarest creature in Greene's fiction, an ordinary man who is not hung up in childhood or adolescence, who is not cynical, who does not flaunt shocking grown-up vices – opium, alcohol, whores, gambling, spying – as badges of maturity. Scobie is not only a good man judged by Greene's grand scale of values; he is also an upright man judged by the petty Victorian scale. He rates both sets of big terms. Yet Greene contrives to live inside him even more credibly and sympathetically than he does inside the whisky priest. How does this happen?

FAREWELL TO ENGLAND

Between *The Power and the Glory* and *The Heart of the Matter*, Greene wrote another 'entertainment', *The Ministry of Fear* (1943). It is one of his less readable books, constructed deliberately to give the effect of a nightmare, with apparently inconsequential actions and phantom-like characters, but, as I have indicated earlier, it is especially interesting to students of the pattern of Greene's mind. The outer action is the German Blitz on London, the final bursting of the boil of European political violence which was festering in the background of all Greene's thrillers of the 1930s. Raven, the international hitman in *A Gun for Sale*, and D., the Spanish Republican agent in

The Confidential Agent, brought the infection home to safe little England; but it was temporarily held at bay with their removal. Now the bombs are falling and London is in flames. Greene had seen it at first hand, as an air-raid warden in the Bloomsbury area, and he wrote the novel a year later while he was in Sierra Leone.

The inner action is the odyssey of the protagonist Rowe from a numbed inertia (anticipating Querry's in *A Burnt-Out Case*) back to childhood innocence and on again to adolescence. Rowe is an acquitted murderer who, after a loss of memory, finds himself under a new name in a shell-shock clinic in the country. The clinic's garden, as we have seen, is based on Uncle Graham's at Harston and contains the pond and island used again in the story about Javitt, 'Under the Garden'. Between the pleasant part of the clinic, where Rowe is recovering, and the unpleasant part, where the violent or difficult patients are housed, is a green baize door. The doctor who owns the clinic is compared to a headmaster and given this description: 'His elderly face under the snow-white hair was hawk-like and noble and a little histrionic, like the portrait of a Victorian' (*MF*, p. 113). He turns out to be part of an enemy spy ring. When Rowe begins to rebel against the doctor's authority he is savagely reminded of his past identity as a murderer and abruptly pushed from childhood into adolescence. He first breaks through the green baize door into the unpleasant part of the clinic and then runs away.

The two actions of the novel – the destruction of the old Victorian security of Britain and the reconstruction and re-destruction of Rowe's Greene-ish childhood – are bound together with the image of romantic adventure stories. Rowe, sleeping in an underground shelter, dreams of talking to his dead mother in another version of Greene's Uncle Graham's Cambridgeshire garden:

'This isn't real life any more. . . . Tea on the lawn, evensong, croquet, the old ladies calling, the gentle unmalicious gossip, the gardener trundling the wheelbarrow full of leaves and grass. . . . I'm wanted for a murder I didn't do. People want to kill me because I know too much. I'm hiding under-ground, and up above the Germans are methodically smashing London to bits all round me. . . . It sounds like a thriller, doesn't it, but the thrillers are like life – more like life than you are, this lawn, your sandwiches, that pine. You used to laugh at the books Miss Savage read – about spies, and murders, and violence, and wild motor-car chases, but dear, that's real life: it's what we've all made of the world since you died.' (*MF*, p. 65)

The book is like a summary of Greene's political thrillers of the 1930s – he says in *Ways of Escape* that it is his 'favourite among what I called then my "entertainments"' – but it contains also a new and significant element. The murder Rowe did do, of which he was acquitted before the opening of the book, was to poison his wife, saving her from a painful illness and a lingering death. Some of the women in Greene's earlier fiction feel pity and responsibility for others – it is part of the superior nature Greene ascribes to them – but few of the men and then only momentarily: Myatt, the Jewish currant merchant in *Stamboul Train*, pities the shivering chorus-girl Coral Musker and lends her his fur coat; Mather, the policeman in *A Gun for Sale*, thinks himself for a moment into the hunted Raven's place; the Assistant Commissioner in *It's a Battlefield*, under his stiff, correct manner, sometimes allows his dutiful responsibility for the safety of London to shade into a responsible pity for the underdog. It is an adult emotion. Adolescents such as Pinkie, Raven or Anthony Farrant and the shabby journalist Minty in *England Made Me* cannot feel it because they are too embedded in their own feelings to imagine someone else's.

But the priest in *The Power and the Glory*, spending a night in gaol and irritated by one of his fellow prisoners, reminds himself that 'when you visualized a man or woman carefully, you could always begin to feel pity. . . . Hate was just a failure of imagination' (*PG*, p. 131). The priest begins by feeling pity mixed with love for his illegitimate daughter, a wretched knowing urchin in one of the poor villages, and the idea grows in his mind until it adds a new dimension to his obscure sense of Christian duty: 'One must love every soul as if it were one's own child. The passion to protect must extend itself over a world' (*PG*, p. 82). The idea clearly grew in Greene's mind too:

39

it chimed with his discovery of Catholicism as an active ingredient in the novels, and it introduced a new perspective on childhood and adolescence, that of the father/headmaster. His use of it in *The Ministry of Fear* is rather mechanical – Rowe is not in any case a character whose emotions can bear any weight for the reader – but Major Scobie in *The Heart of the Matter* might have been invented to embody it.

SCOBIE'S BURDEN

Most of the troubles of Andrews, the hero of Greene's first novel *The Man Within*, stem from his father, a daring and successful smuggler in whose shadow the son is forever judged wanting by the father's shipmates. Thereafter, except for the whisky priest, fathers hardly figure in Greene's fiction. He had children of his own, born in the 1930s, but the relationship never seems to have interested him imaginatively until he came to write *The Heart of the Matter*. His own father died while he was in Sierra Leone. The news came in two telegrams delivered in the wrong order, the first saying his father was dead, the second that he was seriously ill (*SL*, p. 20). Scobie, also in Sierra Leone, receives the news of his daughter's death away in England in the same distressing way.

Greene writes that as a child he resented his father's interest in what he did and that 'only when I had children of my own did I realize how his interest in my doings had been genuine, and only then I discovered a buried love and sorrow for him'. With the news of his father's death he 'unexpectedly felt misery and remorse, remembering how as a young man I had deliberately set out to shock his ideas which had been unflinchingly liberal in politics and gently conservative in morals' (*SL*, p. 20).

Although Scobie's child is dead before *The Heart of the Matter* opens, and his life with his wife Louise is that of a childless marriage, he is pre-eminently a father figure. He first sees his future mistress, Helen Rolt, as hardly more than a child, carried on a stretcher and clutching a stamp album after being saved from a torpedoed ship; and the most moving scene in the book is his keeping watch by another survivor's bed, a 6-year-old girl for whom he makes the shadow of a rabbit on the pillow with his handkerchief and who dies mistaking him for her own drowned father. Just as the priest in *The Power and the Glory* had prayed over his daughter ('O God, give me any kind of death – without contrition, in a state of sin – only save this child'; *PG*, p. 82), so Scobie prays over this substitute child – 'Father, give her peace. Take away my peace for ever, but give her peace' (*HM*, p. 118) – and is also taken at his word. Again, in his public role as deputy commissioner of police, as a headmaster to the community, it is his sympathy with the captain of a Portuguese ship, his connivance in the captain's attempt, against wartime regulations, to smuggle a letter through to his daughter in Germany, that first corrupts him – one thing leading inexorably to another in this tightest of tight plots.

No less a critic and ex-colonial policeman than George Orwell has done a brisk demolition job on this book: its improbable plot, its central Catholic idea ('He appears to share the idea, which has been floating around ever since Baudelaire, that there is something rather *distingué* in being damned') and Scobie himself ('if he were capable of getting into the kind of mess that is described, he would have got into it years earlier').[11]

It is true that the plot, like that of *Othello*, does grate on one with rereading. The plot of *The Power and the Glory*, partly based on the Passion itself – the text is carefully dotted with unmistakable references – and partly on the actual existence of just such a whisky priest, seems natural enough, even if the way one is to read and understand the story is, in Hoggart's term, over-forced; also, as in Greene's previous novels, it relies fairly simply on the mechanism of pursuer and pursued. The difference in *The Heart of the Matter* is that Scobie is pursued solely by the author, partly in the guise of Scobie's own excessive punctilio in matters both human and divine, partly in the exact cueing of outside events to his disadvantage. In *Othello* one cannot help feeling that Shakespeare wants Desdemona and Othello to end up dead on the bed, when one ought to feel that he wants the opposite; similarly with Greene and Scobie. By some particular stretch of the imagination – for he never creates such a character again – he inhabits him, but he also disapproves of him: his character was intended, Greene says in *Ways of Escape*, 'to show that pity can be the expression of an almost monstrous pride' (*WE*, pp. 93–4). So Scobie is condemned for his sense of responsibility, his claim to be soberly grown-up. That such a claim, made not boastfully but with a sensitive diffidence unusual in police administrators or headmasters, should be the single significant cause of his corruption, leading to betrayal, murder, suicide and, in his own eyes, eternal damnation, is a little hard to swallow.

Discussing the effect on him of *The Viper of Milan*, Greene writes: 'Goodness has only once found a perfect incarnation in a human body and never will again, but evil can always find a home there. Human nature is not black and white but black and grey' (*CE*, p. 17). If Satan can always find a home in the world but God only once and that in the past, it is no wonder Scobie is damned. According to the third-century Manichaean heresy, Satan was co-eternal with God; according to the seventeenth-century Jansenists, a Catholic variety of Calvinists, the physical world was given up to evil and only God's elect could find salvation. Greene at the time of *The Heart of the Matter* seems to have been fairly close to both heresies. Marjorie Bowen, he says in the essay 'The Lost Childhood' (1947), 'had given me my pattern – religion might later explain it to me in other terms, but the pattern was already there – perfect evil walking the world where perfect good can never walk again' (*CE*, p. 17). In various interviews since, he has vehemently denied charges of Jansenism or Manichaeism:

> One gets so tired of people saying that my novels are about the opposition of Good and Evil. They are not about Good and Evil, but about human beings.[12]

> Jansenism, you know, believed in the elect – grace came to the elect. . . . I can't imagine anything more unlike my work. I've never believed in hell.[13]

> I find it very difficult to believe in sin. Personally I have very little sense of it.[14]

Is he trying to have it both ways, or has he changed with age? The fact is that Scobie's theological quibbles are only nominally connected with Catholicism; their real connection is with literature, with Shakespeare's Iago or Bowen's Visconti, 'perfect evil walking the world'. For Scobie, though, the evil takes a variety of forms, sometimes inhabiting his conscience, sometimes an actual character such as Wilson, the spy, or the crooked Syrian trader, Yusef. Yusef, incidentally, alludes to that line from Othello's death speech which Greene had quoted in *British Dramatists* as an example of the important things dealt with by the old 'abstract drama': '"I am the base Indian . . . . Who threw away a pearl," Yusef sadly said' (*HM*, p. 192).

Where, then, do we emerge? At a representative of adulthood, a father figure and guardian of the established values of British imperial society, who is destroyed by a Renaissance villain from Greene's adolescence. At the very heart, in fact, of Greene's peculiar 'view of life', which is here, because for once he also inhabits the father, given its counter-view, as if that irritating iconoclast at the head of the column in the Liberian bush had suddenly pulled up his socks and started to look like a real white man. This is why Orwell's down-to-earth strictures are rather beside the point. He could not have written such a novel himself because he could not have conceived of wanting both to understand the steady headmaster and to destroy him in the best tragic manner through his own steadiness. When one reads the book, one wishes that Scobie were not capable of getting into the mess, one wishes that the plot were not so drawn as to catch him at every twist, and one wishes above all that he wouldn't keep insisting on the letter of his Catholic doctrine; but one does not disbelieve in the man himself or indeed in any part of his story. By Orwell's cold light, half the most imaginative novels and plays in the English language could be levelled to the dust. *The Heart of the Matter* is perhaps one of them; it is certainly Greene's best.

Nothing could better illustrate Scobie's distance from Greene's other protagonists than his relationship with his wife Louise. It is, of course, an unhappy relationship, ultimately disastrous, but it is not that of a man to a mirror. The scene of their lunch together before she goes on board the ship for South Africa is remarkable for portraying her feelings as well as his: 'it seemed horrible to both of them that now they would be glad when the separation was complete' (*HM*, p. 95). Louise is not presented as a very lovable person, but she is loved, after his fashion, by Scobie – and he by her, after hers. Greene's theme

43

and plot require that their love should be debased into pity and pathos, but their parting, roughly a third of the way through the book, gives it a dimension he perhaps didn't bargain for: it becomes something other than childhood, idealism, faith or perfect companionship which can be lost; something, in other words, which is obscurely and imperfectly valuable to two people of the opposite sex at the same time. And, although Scobie's mistress is not an objectified character in the way that Louise is, she gains depth from being attached to this stronger relationship. So that inside the existing novel there is almost another, more subtle and perhaps less inexorable, which would have nothing whatever to do with Catholicism or even with the moral values of an upright man, but would explore what one person needs from another.

GOD'S MACHINERY

The End of the Affair (1951) appears at first to be taking up the baton at this point. The protagonist is Bendrix, the unmarried lover, and Scobie has been relegated to his conventional place in Greene's anti-conventional world, as the complaisant husband and complacent civil servant, Henry Miles (he even shares Scobie's first name). But the affair between Henry's wife Sarah and Bendrix is, as the title suggests, only the given starting-point. Greene is still after his 'religious sense', his grand backdrop of heaven and hell, and Catholicism is employed this time as a real *deus ex machina*. God has intervened, or may have intervened, to bring Bendrix back to life after Sarah has found him apparently dead under a fallen door after an air raid. Sarah, having made one of those bargain prayers familiar from *The Power and the Glory* and *The Heart of the Matter*, renounces her liaison with Bendrix and by gradual degrees turns into a miracle-working saint. Bendrix, on the other hand, deserted for no reason he can at first discover, picks up Visconti's ticket:

I have known so intimately the way that demon works in my imagination. . . . He was not Sarah's enemy so much as the enemy of love, and isn't that what the devil is supposed to be? . . . Wouldn't he be afraid that the habit of love might

44

grow, and wouldn't he try to trap us all into being traitors, into helping him extinguish love? (*EA*, p. 58)

The difference here is not that the protagonist represents evil – Raven and Pinkie had done that before – but that he speaks in the first person and hates because he has been dispossessed of love, not because he has never known it. He is also a professional novelist, and the book's structure – folding different sequences of events one within another – is less straightforward than usual.

John Atkins has suggested that '*The End of the Affair* was partly the product of a personal crisis, and the hatred had to be spilled out before Greene could recover his balance',[15] and Greene himself has written that after the war 'the booby-traps I had heedlessly planted in my private life were blowing up in turn' (*WE*, p. 92). But demonic hatred comes better from a ruined childhood than from a frustrated love-affair, and Bendrix often appears more peevish than hating. The most lively part of the book is its detective-story element – the gradual discovery, with the help of a comic sleuth and his boy, of the truth about Sarah's bargain with God. The moment that is over and we are embarked, through the device of Sarah's stolen diary, on Greene's first and last attempt at a female protagonist in the first person, the full hopelessness of the task he has set himself becomes apparent. He cannot imagine what it is like to be a sexually attractive woman, still less how such a woman would fall in love with God. He takes refuge in two of the things he most detests, *Ladies' Magazine* slush and Catholic piety, and hopes that Bendrix's gruff noises will somehow cover his tracks.

The End of the Affair is really the end of the Catholic phase in Greene's fiction, but the Catholic machinery rumbles on a bit. Two rather bogus plays of the 1950s, *The Living Room* and *The Potting Shed*, recycle the religious motifs of *The Heart of the Matter* and *The End of the Affair* respectively: adultery and suicide versus the mercy of God in the first; the bargain prayer which brings a boy back to life at the price of the priest's own faith in the second. Loss of faith is also the issue in 'A Visit to Morin', a story about a bitter old French Catholic writer who, well brandied, tells his young English visitor:

45

'They used to come here in their dozens to see me. I used to get letters saying how I had converted them by this book or that. Long after I ceased to believe myself I was a carrier of belief, like a man can be a carrier of disease without being sick. Women especially. . . . I had only to sleep with a woman to make a convert.' (*SR*, p. 75)

Greene had had some of the same trouble himself after the success of *The Heart of the Matter*:

Never had I received so many letters from strangers – perhaps the majority of them from women and priests. . . . I felt myself used and exhausted by the victims of religion. The vision of faith as an untroubled sea was lost for ever; faith was more like a tempest in which the lucky were engulfed and lost, and the unfortunate survived to be flung battered and bleeding on the shore. (*WE*, pp. 193–4)

Morin suggests, in one of those theological paradoxes of which Greene is so fond, that 'my lack of belief is a final proof that the Church is right and the faith is true. I had cut myself off for twenty years from grace and my belief withered as the priests said it would' (*SR*, p. 78), but he is afraid to test the truth of his argument by receiving the sacraments again. The same notion is propounded by Querry, the protagonist of *A Burnt-Out Case* (1961), in the course of an allegorical story about a king and the royal jeweller who has ceased to believe in the king's existence: 'I'm told that there were moments when he wondered if his unbelief were not after all a final and conclusive proof of the King's existence. This total vacancy might be his punishment for the rules he had wilfully broken' (*BOC*, p. 158).

Frank Kermode, who remarks that 'the best criticism of Greene is hostile' but himself considers *The End of the Affair* a masterpiece, is a stern critic of *A Burnt-Out Case* and especially of Querry's allegory. He sees the theme of Greene's Catholic fiction as the tension between a powerful, unreasonable God and the natural man he has created: 'He has made us as we are and expects us, on terrible penalties, to behave otherwise; He would not leave us in the state of the amoeba, yet He denies us adult brains.' Whereas, according to Kermode, the 'vicious energy of Bendrix' is capable of bearing this tension, the 'rigidly self-conscious despair' of Querry is not.[16]

Kermode is surely bolting the stable door after the horse has fled. *A Burnt-Out Case*, though it is full of Catholics in various states of belief and disbelief, is not about the protagonist's love or hatred for God. Querry is without belief and is not even looking for it. His allegory about the king and the Fabergé-like jeweller, who went on making Easter eggs with crosses on them long after he was bored with his profession, is less about faith than about the use of faith for artistic purposes. It is a weary, and rather wearily written, farewell to that promising box of treasure which Greene unearthed at the time of *Brighton Rock* and *The Lawless Roads*.

3

COMEDY AND POLITICS

People don't laugh much in Greene's novels. When Brown in *The Comedians* asks his favourite whore Tin Tin why she has got on so well with Jones and she replies 'he made me laugh', Brown is taken aback: 'It was a sentence which was to be repeated to me disquietingly in other circumstances. I had learnt in a disorganized life many tricks, but not the trick of laughter' (*C*, p. 150). Querry in *A Burnt-Out Case*, travelling up river to the leper colony, is irritated by 'the too easy laughter' of the Catholic fathers and wonders 'when it was that he had first begun to detest laughter like a bad smell' (*BOC*, p. 15). The obtrusive simile recalls Greene's descriptions of his own schooldays in *A Sort of Life*: 'no servant would have endured the squalor we lived in. . . . a changing room smelling of sweat and stale clothes . . . no moment of the night was free from noise, a cough, a snore, a fart' (*SL*, p. 54). Looking up the passage again, one discovers a footnote. Greene, it seems, had started to write a novel about a school but, revisiting his own and finding it still unbearable, had switched to the Congolese leper colony. Further on, he again mentions 'the odour of farts' and tells us that 'I have disliked the lavatory joke from that age on' (*SL*, p. 59).

His sensitivity to bad smells appears in other novels, especially in descriptions of police stations: 'an appalling smell lay on the air and somebody in the absolute darkness wept' (*PG*, p. 121) and 'the odour of a police station like the ammoniac smell of all zoos the world over' (*OMH*, p. 133) and 'the heavy smell of urine in the air and policemen returning with a smile of satisfaction from the cells' (*C*, p. 93). It is clear that Querry's simile is only a slightly disguised version of Greene's perennial *pensée* about the importance of childhood experience. Bad smells, police cells, school: laughter is associated with adolescent unhappiness (including, no doubt, the mockery of Carter and Watson) in Greene's mind. Wormold, the protagonist of *Our Man in Havana* (1958), reflects that 'Childhood was the germ of all mistrust. You were cruelly joked upon and then you cruelly joked' (*OMH*, p. 31).

In the radio programme *Graham Greene at 75* his old friend Michael Meyer said that 'my main memories are of us roaring with laughter together, of enormous fun', and V. S. Pritchett that 'I have always found him a most engaging man, rather boyish, marvellously fond of a joke and particularly of a practical joke.'[17] Greene is famous for his practical jokes, whether they take the harmless form of entering *New Statesman* competitions with parodies of himself, or the more malicious ones of telephoning strangers in the middle of the night, or persuading the critic Cyril Connolly to wind up a party early and put sheets over all his furniture in the belief that the chimney sweep was going to call first thing in the morning.[18] The dentist husband in the play *The Complaisant Lover* (1959) is a compulsive practical joker, and the lover, Clive, irritated by a trick cigar, suggests that 'jokes like this must be a compensation for something. When we are children we're powerless, and these jokes make us feel superior to our dictators.'[19] In an essay written in 1939, Greene told the story of an elaborate eighteenth-century hoax played on a respectable printseller and speculated whether the victim, 'by his careful prosperity, had aroused the same balked malice of men who sympathize with the defeated and despise the conqueror and dare do nothing but trivial mischief to assert their independence' (*CE*, p. 206). For Greene, evidently, jokes and laughter – like Berkhamsted, like security, like big terms, like things Victorian – are ambivalent: detestable in the mouths of others, but self-assertive and life-giving in one's own, weapons either way.

It is especially significant, then, that Querry dies laughing at himself – the joke being that he, an inveterate adulterer, should be accused of an adultery he has never committed. 'The innocent adulterer,' he says, 'that's not a bad title for a comedy' (*BOC*, p. 193), and, beginning to laugh awkwardly, is shot dead by the aggrieved husband, Rycker, who thinks Querry is laughing at him. In a sense he is, and in a sense Querry's death is semi-suicide; but the point for Greene was not the melodramatic enigma with which he disposed of his burnt-out case but the fact that 'in the course of the blackest book I have written I had discovered Comedy' (*WE*, p. 198). The statement is not strictly true, since he had already written three comedies – *Loser Takes All*, *Our Man in Havana* and *The Complaisant Lover* – as well as the odd comic story; but he means, presumably, that for the first time he had discovered comic as well as tragic elements in the predicament of one of his serious protagonists.

Comedy for Greene is bound up with his antagonism to conventional society. His first attempt at it was a story written in 1940, about a company director whose rumbling stomach imitates an air-raid warning and keeps his fellow directors in an underground shelter for twelve hours (*TOS*, p. 69). It is no more than a ponderous lavatory joke against the bosses. *Loser Takes All* (1955) ends happily, as we have seen, with the protagonist preferring the love of his childlike wife to power and money. The stories in *May We Borrow Your Husband?* (1967) put the boot into, variously, homosexuals of both sexes, a rich woman with a lap-dog, American tourists, bores and a self-important female novelist. *Travels with my Aunt* (1969) is given a certain energy by its game old heroine, and its values are momentarily complicated at the end by her connivance in the death of the faithful black lover Wordsworth (reminiscent of Scobie's treachery towards his servant Ali), but it is really only an extended sneer at the law-abiding and ordinary as compared with the adventurous and criminal. As for *Doctor Fischer of Geneva* (1980), it can hardly be called comedy at all, except that it takes the form of a series of practical jokes and is concerned primarily with the discomfiture of the rich and successful; nevertheless it demonstrates in an extreme form why Greene's straight comedy is so unsatisfactory. He is not interested in the observation of human behaviour but in proving a point and preaching a moral. Thus the characters in his comedies are dummies, the tone is uneasily derisive, if not actually vengeful, and the conclusion foregone.

The truth is that Greene has never brought himself to consider sex or money as serious subjects. For him they are trivial and worldly diversions which do not strike, to use an image of his own, 'the fork of his imagination' (*CE*, p. 47). 'What poetry would be left in life', asks Raffles, the aristocratic burglar in Greene's play *The Return of A. J. Raffles* (1975), 'if one couldn't feel fear?'[20] 'Poetry' in Greene's vocabulary always refers to content rather than form and is a word of approbation meaning imaginative passion or excitement, something beyond the scope of merely rational, realistic, social writers. 'Henry James was a poet and Defoe was not,' he writes (*CE*, p. 67), and again: 'Fielding had tried to make the novel poetic, even though he himself had not the poetic mind, only a fair, a generous and a courageous mind' (*CE*, p. 74). 'Poetry' for Greene is the literary expression of 'the religious sense', and it is clearly not to be found in social or domestic comedy. Oddly enough, though, the Raffles play is his only successful soufflé, probably because its hero is an absurd Victorian adventurer and its form farce rather than comedy. The author, relaxing in a childlike aristocratic atmosphere dominated by 'Mr Portland', the pseudonymous Prince of Wales, is able for once to rise above his angry disapproval of the beastly bourgeois and simply amuse himself.

The comedy he discovered at the end of *A Burnt-Out Case* is different. It came from the incompatibility, which he didn't at first notice, between his protagonist as he emerged in the writing of the book and the role that had been originally assigned to him. Querry was intended to be a tragic figure in the line of Greene's other Catholic heroes, though suffering from an even more extreme failure to live up to his own intimations of metaphysical purpose, the complete loss of his faith. But, no doubt because his own difficulties with his Catholic beliefs were associated with his popular success as a 'Catholic' novelist, Greene chose to make Querry a successful man, a world-famous Catholic architect and incidentally a successful Don Juan too. This effectively torpedoed the original idea; for whether or not Querry's worldly success was the result of his loss of faith (his pact with the Devil), or the cause of it, or quite independent of it, his 'hollowness' in the novel is expressed in terms of his losing the taste for life – for architecture, fame and women – not in terms of losing a belief in God. Thus Querry comes out on the wrong side of Greene's 'view of life', metaphysically and therefore 'poetically' deficient, associated with sex, money and the values of conventional society, a comic not a tragic hero.

51

So he dies laughing at his own and life's absurdity. So Greene recognizes that, if he cannot any longer conscientiously include God and the Devil in his fiction, he will have to make a new pact with the world, reduce the pretensions of his protagonists from tragedy to tragicomedy and himself retreat to a more detached, ironic position. Don Quixote, the absurd romantic, must become the model in place of Faust and Don Juan. 'At the end of a long journey,' he writes in *Ways of Escape*, 'without knowing myself the course which I had been taking, I found myself, in "A Visit to Morin" and *A Burnt-Out Case*, in that tragi-comic region of La Mancha where I expect to stay' (*WE*, p. 198).

In his most recent novel, *Monsignor Quixote* (1982), Greene actually transposes elements of Cervantes' novel directly into the modern world, retaining the La Mancha setting and alluding to some of the original incidents. Don Quixote himself becomes a comically innocent parish priest, his horse Rocinante a battered little Seat car and his squire Sancho Panza a communist ex-mayor. But Greene parts company with his original in altering the books of chivalry that drove Don Quixote mad into Monsignor Quixote's library of favourite Christian authors – St John of the Cross, St Teresa, St Francis de Sales and the Gospels, the holiest and best, as it were – for Cervantes, of course, took a dim view of his foolish hero's romantic reading-matter, whereas Greene wholly approves of his priest and his priest's books. The basic theme of *Monsignor Quixote* is the same as Dostoevsky's in the 'Grand Inquisitor' section of *The Brothers Karamazov*, that anyone who goes about the world behaving as Christ and his true followers did is liable to seem mad and dangerous to most people, but especially so to the princes and bureaucrats of the Catholic Church. In Greene's version the foolish books are not those admired by his hero but certain works of moral theology endorsed by his persecutors, the church authorities, and in particular a book by Father Heribert Jone which, among other absurdities, states that the unexpected arrival of a third person makes *coitus interruptus* permissible. Thus *Monsignor Quixote* is partly designed to score off officially pious Catholics, rather as *Travels with my Aunt* was aimed at bourgeois secular respectability.

The theme is broadened, through the discussions between the Catholic Quixote and the communist Sancho, so as to link the insensitivity and authoritarianism of the organized church to those of organized Marxism: Sancho is a 'good' communist as Quixote is a 'good' Christian, and they are clearly closer in many ways to each other than either is to his nominal party. The journeys they make through a Spain only recently liberated from Franco's dictatorship distantly recall the pursuits, in grimmer circumstances, of previous Greene protagonists; and although, in the gentler climate of freshly sprung democracy, Greene allows this pair a holiday spirit of simple pleasures (good companionship, country wine and plain fare) he has his pack of evil hounds on leash ready to hunt them down for their nonconformism. To admirers of Greene's more substantial work, however, the Monsignor's exaggerated unworldliness, mild escapades and well-worn Greenean *pensées* ('Oh Sancho, Sancho, it's an awful thing not to have doubts') are likely to appear almost shockingly cosy, in spite of the violent finale. The general tone of the book – autumnal, pastoral, elegiac – is in great contrast to that of its predecessor, the icily savage satire on capitalism, *Doctor Fischer*, though that too – in its treatment of the young lovers – was distinctly soft at the centre.

One of the most admirable and characteristic things about Greene is the way that he has constantly sought to escape from the straitjacket of his own success – to practise his own preaching against the boredom and corruption of a settled life – by expanding his repertoire, both with new modes of fiction and with excursions into other forms of writing – plays, film scripts, short stories, essays, travel books, biography and autobiography. But, twist and turn as he may, a writer can no more disguise – least of all from himself – his distinctive voice, the pattern of his mind, than he can alter his fingerprints. Greene in La Mancha is still unmistakably Greene, but it is not a region that brings out the best in him as a novelist. Tragicomedy requires an artist with a light touch and an eye for shades of grey; Greene takes the world hard and sees it in terms of sharply defined antitheses and antagonisms.

THE CHROMIUM WORLD

By entering Greene's La Mancha in the wake of *A Burnt-Out Case*, we have got far ahead of his chronological development.

A Burnt-Out Case, the coda to Greene's group of Catholic novels (though *Monsignor Quixote* now forms a kind of second coda), is itself displaced in Greene's development, since by 1961 when it was published he had already written the first two of a new group of political novels. In spite of being set in the Belgian Congo with occasional noises off anticipating the political violence to come, *A Burnt-Out Case* is too concentrated on Querry's troubles to be considered part of this group, which stems originally from *The Power and the Glory* and *The Lawless Roads*. Greene's visit to Mexico was his first experience of the Third World as a political arena. His pre-war thrillers, culminating in *The Ministry of Fear* during the war, were set against the European political upheaval of the period, and it was not until after the war was over that what he had seen in Mexico as a local episode of anti-Catholic oppression began to take its place in a wider context.

The old European empires were breaking up and the new American empire was coming into being, against some competition from the USSR. Greene's anti-Americanism is notorious, but it derives from further back than America's record in the Third World; it is really an extension of his dislike for the suburban Protestant materialism of England, and is already apparent in the film criticism he wrote for the *Spectator* in the 1930s:

> The American *Crime and Punishment* ... is a dreadful contrast to the French. In the dark intense French picture there was at least something of Dostoievsky's religious and unhappy mind. This gleaming lunch-bar-chromium version – which opens at the University with Raskolnikov receiving his degree and listening to the Vice-Chancellor's earnest American abstractions about Youth and Alma Mater and the Future – is vulgar as only the great New World can be vulgar, with the vulgarity of the completely irreligious, of sentimental idealism, of pitch-pine ethics, with the hollow optimism about human nature, of a salesman who has never failed to sell his canned beans.[21]

In Mexico his prejudice was confirmed: 'I loathed Mexico, but there were times when it seemed as if there were worse places. . . . the drugstore and the Coca-Cola, the hamburger, the sinless graceless chromium world' (*LR*, p. 184). He was still in Mexico when the libel suit brought·against him by the child-star Shirley Temple and Twentieth Century Fox came to court in London. In a review in *Night and Day* Greene had suggested that, as he puts it in *Ways of Escape*, 'she had a certain adroit coquetry which appealed to middle-aged men' (*WE*, p. 47). The case was settled out of court, Greene apologized and paid damages, *Night and Day* ceased publication and Hollywood might be said to have had its revenge for all his barbed comments in the past. After that, the case of Graham Greene versus the USA was adjourned until 1954 when, because of his brief association with the Communist Party as an Oxford undergraduate, he was refused a visa to enter the United States and deported, much to his delight, from Puerto Rico. A year later he published *The Quiet American* (1955), based on the French colonial war in Vietnam, which he had witnessed as a journalist; the villains of the book, however, were not the French, still less the Vietnamese, but the already covertly interfering Americans.

The character of Alden Pyle, the quiet American, objectifies a by now familiar emotional tangle. He is at once the hero of a Victorian adventure story – brave, gentle, idealistic, chivalrous, innocent – and the son of a New England professor of science with gold-rimmed glasses; 'gold rims, like a pipe, always give me the impression of a rectitude I can never achieve,' says the narrator of a story in *May We Borrow Your Husband?* (*MWB*, p. 114). The brisk, dismissive portrait of Pyle's father, who does not appear as a character but is said to be 'the world authority on underwater erosion' and to have had his picture on the cover of *Time* (*QA*, p. 30), reminds one that Greene's feud with materialism looks forward as well as back. Much as he dislikes the social edifices of his own father's generation, he allies himself with that generation in disliking the cultural edifices of his own. As far back as *Stamboul Train* he was deriding Mr Eckman's steel chairs and 'bright steely room' (*ST*, pp. 205–6). Krogh, the half-pathetic, half-devilish financier in *England Made Me*, lives in a glass and steel office block with a sculpture in the courtyard which he can't understand but feels is suitable to his image as a king of the modern world. The hero of *Loser Takes All*, temporarily rich from his casino winnings, reflects that 'I had enough now to buy a partnership in some safe modest business without walls of glass and modern sculpture' (*LTA*, p. 78). Wormold in *Our Man in Havana* considers that at school 'his edges had been chipped, but the result had not, he thought, been character – only shapelessness, like an exhibit in the Museum of Modern Art' (*OMH*, p. 31). Most telling of all, the odious Dr Percival in *The Human Factor* tries to explain the virtues of an abstract painting by Ben Nicholson to Colonel Daintry (a character Greene approves of) and to use it as an illustration of how Daintry should go about his unpleasant job of singling out a spy in the department:

> 'You've no responsibility for what happens in the blue or red squares. In fact not even in the yellow. You just report. No bad conscience. No guilt. . . . Do just try to understand that picture. . . . If you could only see it with my eyes, you would sleep well tonight.' (*HF*, pp. 38–9)

In just Dr Percival's spirit of keeping the squares separate, Alden Pyle comes to work undercover at the American Embassy in Saigon. His mission is to combat the totalitarian nightmare of communism, but his method is to supply plastic bombs to a Vietnamese 'Third Force' which uses them to blow up ordinary Vietnamese in the streets. That Greene sees Dr Percival's and Pyle's spirit as peculiarly American is confirmed by a remark in *The Third Man* (1950): 'American chivalry is always, it seems to me, carefully canalized – one still awaits the American saint who will kiss a leper's sores' (*TM*, p. 94). It is a British policeman speaking, another of those mature, chivalrous men of the old world – the Assistant Commissioner, Mather, Scobie, Daintry and Vigot, the French policeman in *The Quiet American* – whom Greene somewhat reluctantly respects. Pyle's heroic qualities are undercut by his immature inability to envisage consequences, his lack of imagination and his capacity for swallowing half-baked ideas. He is, in fact, a lethal combination of Pinkie from *Brighton Rock* with American 'pitch-pine ethics'.

But Pyle is not the protagonist. He is viewed through the eyes of a British journalist, Fowler, the first of three such uncommitted protagonist/narrators – Brown in *The Comedians* and Dr

Plarr in *The Honorary Consul* are the others – who are perched on the edge of America's brave new world. Fowler's story in some ways parallels Bendrix's in *The End of the Affair*. Bendrix's mistress is stolen by God, Fowler's by Pyle; and both stories are by way of being confessions of inadequacy, told moreover by the same device of enfolding the past in the present and in a similar aggressive manner which masks the real feelings of the narrator. Bendrix professes to hate God, but prays to him at the end; Fowler brings about Pyle's ambush and murder by the communists, but wishes afterwards that 'there existed someone to whom I could say that I was sorry' (*QA*, p. 187). The difference, and improvement, in *The Quiet American* is that perfect goodness no longer unbalances the choice, and Fowler is required to take the more doubtful measure of humanity. 'Sooner or later,' the communist Heng tells Fowler after he has arranged to betray Pyle to his enemies, 'one has to take sides. If one is to remain human' (*QA*, p. 172). Fowler's humanity is rather more complicated than that: it consists in taking the side of the murdered Vietnamese as against Pyle and his American bosses, but also in retrospect taking Pyle's side against his (Fowler's) own sexual jealousy and cowardly betrayal to the communists. In this way Greene separates what is good about Pyle (the adventure-story hero part of him) from what is bad (the American materialism). Fowler is not really uncommitted at all; he is committed to Javitt's brand of disloyalty, which is given its political definition by Wormold, the protagonist of Greene's next Third World novel, *Our Man in Havana* (1958):

'I wouldn't kill for my country. I wouldn't kill for capitalism or Communism or social democracy or the welfare state – whose welfare? I would kill Carter because he killed Hasselbacher. A family feud had been a better reason for murder than patriotism or the preference for one economic system over another. If I love or if I hate, let me love or hate as an individual. I will not be 59200/5 in anyone's global war.' (*OMH*, p. 186)

Neither Fowler himself nor his situation is at all comic, but Wormold and his are. At this stage, before he had found the comic spot in Querry, Greene could only associate comedy with a character on the conventional side of society. So Wormold is a blameless tradesman, selling vacuum cleaners in Havana; and the comedy consists in his being recruited as a British secret agent and having to invent the material for his reports. The comedy indeed turns sour, and *Our Man in Havana* becomes the last of Greene's thrillers or 'entertainments'; but Wormold, like the accountant in *Loser Takes All* and Henry Pulling in *Travels with my Aunt*, is essentially a cipher. In so far as they rebel against their stated natures and occupations, these characters amuse their author and take on a little reflected energy from the sudden change in their circumstances – even begin to behave remarkably unlike their former selves and more like Greene's other protagonists – but they lack depth for him, since they have not been schooled to unhappiness.

BANANA POLITICS

After *A Burnt-Out Case* and his glimpse of La Mancha, Greene began to build again on Fowler and produced, in *The Comedians*, Brown. *A Burnt-Out Case* is theoretically concerned with varieties of religious faith and its absence, and has a carefully graded cast of subsidiary characters: the Father Superior is a 'good' believer, while Father Thomas and the predatory pietist Rycker are 'bad' believers; Dr Colin is a 'good' atheist, while the popular journalist Parkinson represents vulgar materialism. But, in *The Comedians* (1966), the characters are graded with rather more subtlety by their degrees of political involvement: in the background, power is held by the purely evil Doc Duvalier and his henchmen, the Tontons Macoute, and feebly challenged by the 'good' but impractical guerrillas; nearer the foreground are the idealized Dr Magiot, a Haitian Marxist version of Dr Colin, and the almost impossibly innocent and unworldly – though still materialist – American vegetarians, Mr and Mrs Smith. In practice, as we have seen, Querry didn't really fit the theoretical framework of *A Burnt-Out Case*. Brown, though, the hotelier with a chequered past, who was educated by the Jesuits but has no faith, who was initiated into sex the same day as he was initiated into gambling, whose father is unknown and whose

58

mother is 'an accomplished comedian', is perfectly at home in the setting provided for him. Brown is Greene's definitive protagonist:

> The rootless have experienced, like all the others, the tempt-ation of sharing the security of a religious creed or a political faith, and for some reason we have turned the temptation down. We are the faithless; we admire the dedicated, the Doctor Magiots and the Mr Smiths for their courage and their integrity, for their fidelity to a cause, but through timidity, or through lack of sufficient zest, we find ourselves the only ones truly committed – committed to the whole world of evil and of good, to the wise and to the foolish, to the indifferent and to the mistaken. We have chosen nothing except to go on living, 'rolled round on Earth's diurnal course, With rocks and stones and trees'. (C, p. 279)

The Comedians appears to rebut the point I made earlier. It is a tragicomedy and it is one of Greene's best novels. The reason is almost certainly the setting, which, however toned down the characters may be by comparison with those in previous books, itself supplies the hard edges and lurid colours that Greene requires for his most successful compositions. Greene's Haiti is a very long way from Cervantes' La Mancha. La Mancha is a relatively ordinary and pleasant part of the world, whereas Haiti is a region of hell; Don Quixote is a childish madman, whereas Brown is neither childish nor mad. In fact he has more in common with Sancho Panza. The obvious Don Quixote in *The Comedians* is Mr Smith, who once stood as a presidential candidate in the USA and has come to Haiti to set up a vegetarian centre; but halfway between Smith and Brown, and forming a triumvirate with them, stands an extra character called 'Major' Jones, a less successful and more pathetic con-man than Brown. Jones does not survive the story – he is betrayed by vanity rather than dedication into joining the guerrillas, and dies the military hero he always claimed to be. But, although Brown helps bring about Jones's death (and with the same sexual motive as Fowler brings about Pyle's), he is really absolved of the responsibility by the fact that Jones is himself enough of a 'comedian' to have known better. One is reminded of the early story 'When Greek Meets Greek', in which a con-man pretending to be a peer sends his son to a fake Oxford college set up by another con-man (*TOS*, pp. 47–61).

Greene's difficulty, because his childhood and adolescence loom so large for him, has always been to create an adult protagonist. He succeeded with the headmasterly Scobie, but awkwardly and against the grain, and could not resist pulling the alien creature down. His natural idea of being adult is of a kind of adolescent promotion into the forbidden self-indulgences of alcohol and sex, opium and cynicism. Brown is just such an adult, a withered adolescent, as it were, but much of that side of him devolves on Jones, and the contrast gives Brown a distinct appearance of maturity. There is the contrast too with Haiti. Brown *returns* to Haiti – it is indeed the nearest thing he has to a home – but such a society, ruled by superstition, corruption and terror, makes his brand of irresponsibility look almost like reliability. He cannot recognize Mr Smith's big terms, 'Mankind, Justice, the Pursuit of Happiness'; but he can respect Mr Smith, even though he is an American of exaggerated moral rectitude, for his opposition to Haitian chaos. In a European or American setting Brown would rate as a gipsy and outlaw; in Haiti he is willy-nilly on the side of order and good government.

Dr Plarr in *The Honorary Consul* (1973) is a still more settled version of Brown, pursuing peace and quiet in a forgotten corner of Argentina. He indulges in a little promiscuous sex, but otherwise he is a minor pillar of the community. His Jones is the British honorary consul Charlie Fortnum, kidnapped in mistake for the American ambassador by a group of Paraguayan terrorists with whom Plarr is in contact – his own father being a prisoner in a Paraguayan gaol. As in all Greene's stories, the plot has its own momentum, but here the characters are pallid, and the long static scene of discussion and argument between the kidnappers and their hostages – for Plarr too is eventually detained in their slum hideout – which takes up nearly a quarter of the book is strangely ill judged. Greene is usually more crafty at spicing his moral discourse with action.

Plarr lacks energy, no doubt partly because the situation does not call it out of him. Bumbling old Charlie Fortnum and the argumentative terrorists – led by a conscience-stricken

ex-priest, shadow of the priest in *The Power and the Glory* –
are no substitutes for the ever-fugitive, ever-hopeful Jones and
the vicious Tontons Macoute who support Brown in his role as
the surviving comedian. The only really lively character in *The
Honorary Consul* is quite incidental to the plot: the local writer
Jorge Julio Saavedra, who begins as a take-off of all those Latin
American writers obsessed with *machismo*, but develops into a
figure quite new to Greene. Saavedra's dapper, old-fashioned
appearance and manner suggest to Dr Plarr that he lives 'in
some old colonial house with barred windows looking out on a
shady street'. The reality is a small, barely furnished flat on the
third floor of a shabby modern block. Greene, speaking
through Dr Plarr, permits himself a kind of tribute to all the less
successful members of his own profession:

> His obsession with literature was not absurd whatever the
> quality of his books. He was willing to suffer poverty for its
> sake, and disguised poverty was far worse to endure than an
> open one. The effort needed to polish his shoes, to press the
> suit. . . . He couldn't, like the young, let things go. Even his
> hair must be cut regularly. A missing button would reveal
> too much. Perhaps he would be remembered in the history of
> Argentine literature only in a footnote, but he would have
> deserved his footnote. The bareness of the room could be
> compared to the inextinguishable hunger of his literary
> obsession. (*HC*, p. 164)

Greene seldom allows his characters, except those like Dr
Colin and Dr Magiot whom he unequivocally admires, this
sort of dignity. The fact that he can allow it to an otherwise
ridiculous character is some measure of Plarr's difference from
previous protagonists: he is more objective, less self-obsessed.
The fact that this also makes him less interesting tells us a good
deal about Greene's peculiarity as a novelist. Unlike, say, his
contemporary Anthony Powell, whose narrator in *A Dance to
the Music of Time* acts as a clear glass through which one can
see the multifarious shapes and colours of his characters,
Greene moulds and colours his subsidiary characters entirely
by reference to his narrator/protagonist. This is what, extended
to things and places as well as characters, makes critics talk of
'Greeneland'.

4

THE MAN WITHIN

GREENELAND

The idea of Greeneland irritates Greene:

> 'This is Indo-China,' I want to exclaim, 'this is Mexico, this is Sierra Leone carefully and accurately described. I have been a newspaper correspondent as well as a novelist. I assure you that the dead child lay in the ditch in just that attitude. In the canal of Phat Diem the bodies stuck out of the water . . .'
> (*WE*, p. 60)

Of course he is right. The observed details in his novels are carefully and accurately described, or at least in the two cases by which one can best judge – the documentary *The Lawless Roads* compared with *The Power and the Glory*, and *Congo Journal* compared with *A Burnt-Out Case* – they are carefully and accurately transcribed from the notebook to the resulting novel. After the failure of *The Name of Action* and *Rumour at Nightfall*, Greene deliberately turned to realism. The beginning of *Stamboul Train* was, he tells us, meticulously researched from a third-class window, though he travelled only as far as Cologne (*WE*, p. 23). *It's a Battlefield* and *A Gun for Sale* are equally scrupulous with the topography of London and Nottingham, and he travelled specially to Sweden for the background to *England Made Me*.

But the critics are right too. Greeneland is not the original landscape; it is the way a landscape is distorted as in a heat haze by the view of life projected on to it. The facts may be never so accurate in themselves; but they are selected and placed in order to contribute to what one might call the prevailing Greenery. Richard Hoggart, in his essay 'The Force of Caricature', has noted how Greene 'uses the selectively typical catalogue as much as Auden' and quotes this example from *Brighton Rock* (*BR*, p. 57):

He looked with contempt down the narrow hall – the shell-case converted into an umbrella-stand, the moth-eaten stag's head bearing on one horn a bowler hat, a steel helmet used for ferns. . . . He lit the gas fire, turned on a stand lamp in a red silk shade with a bobble fringe. The light glowed on a silver-plated biscuit box, a framed wedding-group.[22]

Hoggart considers the detail 'all too typical – we are in the world of *New Statesman* competitions'; but this is surely unfair. There would have been no such *New Statesman* competition if Greene had not invented it. The voice is his, even if there is an element of caricature in the narrowness of the viewpoint, the dominance of the authorial protagonist. It is a style one can grow tired of, especially when, as in *The Honorary Consul*, it has grown a little tired of itself; however, if one objects to it, it should not be because one finds it false to one's own experience, or to the perhaps broader experience of other writers, but only because one suspects it is false to Greene's.

There are occasions when one does suspect it, especially in those too self-conscious similes which are Greene's most obvious method of colouring the landscape with his protagonist's feelings:

The Boy took his brandy and drank it down; he coughed when it took him by the throat, it was like the stain of the world in his stomach. (*BR*, p. 232)

D. climbed into an empty carriage after Jarvis and saw the porter, the general waiting-room, the ugly iron foot-bridge, the signalman holding a cup of tea, go backwards like peace. (*CA*, p. 159)

A big wardrobe stood open and two white suits hung there like the last teeth in an old mouth. (*OMH*, pp. 138–9)

In *The Lawless Roads* his own feelings colour the landscape in this description of a 2-year-old asleep in her nurse's arms:

her tiny ears already drilled for rings and a gold bangle round the little bony wrists – handcuffed to sophistication at birth – like goodness dying out in the hot seaport. (*LR*, p. 99)

This is certainly Greene at his worst, trading on a cheap patent emotion. He was always tempted, he tells us in *A Sort of Life*, by exaggerated similes; he and his wife used to call them 'leopards' – after a particularly glaring example in *The Man Within*. Yet one can quote good 'leopards' as well as bad, especially those which compare concrete to concrete and are touched with humour:

> He had very limited small talk, and his answers fell like trees across the road. (*EA*, p. 171)

> 'Ha, ha.' Father Thomas caught the joke in mid-air and confiscated it, like a schoolboy's ball, under his soutane. (*BOC*, p. 92)

> Once a beautiful little green snake moved across the path, upright, bearing her bust proudly forward into the grasses like a hostess painted by Sargent, poisonous with gentility, a Fabergé jewel. (*JWM*, p. 141)

But, regardless of the occasional lapses or felicities, the highly recognizable, easily parodied style is all of a piece with everything else discussed in this study: the obsession with childhood and adolescence, the authorial protagonists, the division of the characters into 'good' gipsies and 'bad' stay-at-homes, the tightly controlled plots and the romantic desire for some added significance to human actions, whether it be 'the religious sense' or the political sense. The question is, do we, like Hoggart, 'find the novels up to a point arresting because they are forceful, melodramatic presentations of an obsessed and imaginative personality',[23] or can we go further and say that, however tightly controlled they are by the author and however peculiar to his individual circumstances, they also express something more general? Clearly they do, or the Catholic novels, for example, would not have meant so much to so many; equally clearly, Greene himself is suspicious of this kind of success. He even suggests that 'there must have been something corrupt' in *The Heart of the Matter*, 'for the book appealed too often to weak elements in its readers' (*WE*, p. 193).

But isn't this exactly what is general about all his books? They appeal to weak elements – by which Greene presumably means lack of self-confidence, loss of faith and hope, the sense of failure, the need for advice and authority – because they are about such weak elements. Their model is the Victorian adventure story – but translated to a world in which the Victorian adventure hero cannot rely on the values that once supported him. Indeed, he is on his honour to be disloyal to them. What, then, is left? A catalogue of personal weaknesses, a plot which plays on those weaknesses, a style which extends them to places, things and other characters, and an outcome which is in the world's terms a defeat: execution for the priest, death by shooting for Querry and Plarr, suicide for Scobie, ironic survival as an undertaker's assistant for Brown.

Of course, in the code of Greene's view of life, one can read a kind of 'glory' into these endings, but it is the glory of obscure martyrdom in a struggle fought mainly with one's own weaknesses. Even if the story is still a kind of adventure yarn, the hero has lost almost all trace of adventurousness. Rowe in *The Ministry of Fear*

> was no longer capable of sacrifice, courage, virtue, because he no longer dreamed of them. He was aware of the loss – the world had dropped a dimension and become paper-thin. He wanted to dream, but all he could practise now was despair . . . (*MF*, p. 73)

In an essay written in 1951, Greene discusses Rider Haggard's friendship with Kipling:

> Fishing together for trout at Bateman's, these two elderly men – in some ways the most successful writers of their time . . . suddenly let out the secret. 'I happened to remark', Haggard wrote, 'that I thought this world was one of the hells. He replied that he did not think it – he was certain of it. He went on to show that it had every attribute of hell; doubt, fear, pain, struggle, bereavement, almost irresistible temptations springing from the nature with which we are clothed, physical and mental suffering, etc. ending in the worst fate man can devise for man, Execution!' (*CE*, pp. 159–60)

So Greene legitimizes his own reaction against Victorian strength and certainty in the mouths of two of his apparently most confident Victorian predecessors. But, if he resents the fact that so many readers find their own truth in his pages and even look to him as a kind of surrogate priest who understands their plight better than real priests, it can only be because – though the passing of time has made his once subversive view of life rather widespread and acceptable – he still clings to the romantic dream of being outcast and alone.

BERKHAMSTED REVISITED

The Human Factor was begun and temporarily abandoned more than ten years before it was published in 1978. In 1963 Kim Philby, the 'Third Man' in the Burgess and Maclean affair, defected to the Soviet Union. In 1968 Philby's autobiography *My Silent War* was reviewed by Greene, who had once been his subordinate in the Secret Service. The review, although it noted in its subject 'the sharp touch of the icicle in the heart', was calculated to raise British hackles: 'who among us has not committed treason to something or someone more important than a country?' and 'my old liking for him comes back' and 'after thirty years in the underground surely he had earned his right to a rest' (*CE*, pp. 311–14). Greene insists in *Ways of Escape* that Maurice Castle, the protagonist of *The Human Factor*, bears no resemblance in character or motive to Philby. Nor does he. Castle is both a less important spy and a more retiring person than Philby, and he is motivated not by ideological commitment to the cause of Soviet communism but by hatred of South African apartheid and the covert support given to it by the British and American governments. In choosing such a subject, Greene was making use of his own rather out-of-date experience of Secret Service work, and at the same time finding home ground again in the story of a man who is a real outlaw, with every man's hand against him and only his own tenuous sense of justification to sustain him in a dark wood of doubts and fears. We are back in the costume partly of the priest in *The Power and the Glory* (Castle is somewhat addicted to whisky), partly of Andrews, the hero of *The Man Within* (though he was a traitor to his outlaw comrades rather than to his country), who drew such strength, faith and hope as he could command from his *princesse lointaine*, Elizabeth. Castle's *princesse* is his black South African wife, Sarah; and Greene is no more able to give her reality than he was Elizabeth, nearly fifty years earlier. However, Castle himself – colourless, outwardly conventional, *homo suburbanus* even to his final retreat in a Moscow flat – marks both the distance travelled from Greene's first novel to this late one, and the circularity of the journey.

There is nothing romantic about Castle, except the fact of his being a double agent; he is not even, like D., Wormold or Pulling, a worm that turns and takes the action into his own hands – all he does is to relax into the helping hands of his Soviet masters. There are no noticeable 'leopards'. As for the preoccupation with failure, which was Andrews's chief motivating force, it has been reduced to this:

> Why are some of us, he wondered, unable to love success or power or great beauty? Because we feel unworthy of them, because we feel more at home with failure? He didn't believe that was the reason. Perhaps one wanted the right balance, just as Christ had, that legendary figure whom he would have liked to believe in. . . . He was there to right the balance. That was all. (*HF*, p. 147)

Is this really Greene? The religious sense reduced to a purely humanistic 'balance'? Failure something felt in others, not in oneself? Castle, of course, is a successful spy, even though he is being used by the Russians for a purpose he is unaware of.

But the change is most marked in the setting. It is Berkhamsted: the Berkhamsted of ordinary schoolmasters and suburban commuters, not of the 'rich' or 'intellectual' Greenes. Over the door of Castle's house is the stained-glass window of the Laughing Cavalier which Greene describes in *A Sort of Life* as belonging to his childhood dentist (*SL*, p. 28) and behind which he suffered his first experience of pain. Dentists and teeth are a minor leitmotif in Greene's work. *The Power and the Glory* opens with a description of Mr Tench the dentist waiting for his ether cylinder, and ends – or nearly so – with him drilling the teeth of the Chief of Police while the priest is shot in the courtyard below (*PG*, pp. 7, 216). Mr Tench is based on the American dentist Greene met in Mexico:

> without a memory and without a hope in the immense heat, he loomed during those days as big as a symbol – I am not

sure of what, unless the aboriginal calamity, 'having no hope, and without God in the world'. (*LR*, p. 127)[24]

Yusef, the villainous Syrian in *The Heart of the Matter*, has gold teeth – always, like gold-rimmed glasses, a bad sign in Greene – fitted by his dentist brother; so does Jones's Tonton Macoute driver in *The Comedians*. The practical-joking husband in *The Complaisant Lover* is a dentist, and the appalling Dr Fischer in *Doctor Fischer of Geneva* made his millions out of toothpaste. In *The Human Factor* itself, Colonel Daintry and Dr Percival, the two investigators trying to track down the double agent in Castle's department, compare the virtues of Daintry's electric water-pick with Percival's old-fashioned toothpick from Cartier's (gold, of course, since Percival is the villain; *HF*, p. 37).

The Laughing Cavalier over Castle's door perhaps stands for the pain and loss hanging over this apparently secure' retreat; but he also seems to be there as a kind of exorcism, just as the common where Greene hid when he ran away from school, and where he later played his notorious games of Russian roulette with his brother's revolver, is used by Castle as a 'drop' for his Soviet contact. Berkhamsted, though it is also Castle's birthplace, is given to him not as a place where a peculiarly sensitive child first learnt to distinguish heaven from hell but as an absolutely neutral English town, since 'in a bizarre profession anything which belongs to an everyday routine gains great value' (*HF*, p. 17).

In the end, though, as a character in one of Ivy Compton-Burnett's novels remarks, 'A leopard does not change his spots or change his feeling that spots are rather a credit.' Greene may be laying his own childhood to rest; turning his back on the 'religious sense' and even, by locating it offstage in Castle's past, the political sense; giving his protagonist a flawlessly happy marriage with his *princesse lointaine*; making him a loving father to his adopted son; setting the scene in the London and suburbs of ordinary civil servants; doing everything on the surface to deny the existence of Greeneland and suppress the growth of Greenery: yet the familiar patterns break through as the story progresses. There is a Visconti/Iago figure in the shape of Dr Percival, whose unsavoury admiration for Ben Nicholson's abstract painting prepares the watchful reader for his role as a Jacobean poisoner; there is Colonel Daintry, the 'good' policeman in the line of the Assistant Commissioner, Mather, Scobie and Vigot; there is Boris, the Soviet control, the only person to whom Castle can unburden himself, who is specifically compared to a Catholic priest – 'a man who received one's confession whatever it might be without emotion' (*HF*, p. 117); and there is Castle's office colleague Davis, whose dream of at last giving some modest shape and stability to his hitherto desultory life is brutally disrupted. He belongs to a group that includes Coral Musker in *Stamboul Train*, Conrad Drover in *It's a Battlefield*, Anthony Farrant in *England Made Me*, Else, the hotel maid in *The Confidential Agent*, and Jones in *The Comedians*. They are the innocent bystanders in Greene's war between good and evil, natural gipsies, but too vulnerable and unselfconscious to qualify as true comedians. They can be recognized by their fatal capacity for hope. Any Greene character who builds even a modest castle in Spain (whether in the form of Jones's dream of creating a Caribbean golf paradise called Sahib House, or Davis's of becoming our man in Lourenço Marques) is certain, sooner rather than later, to be kicked in the teeth.

The 'human factor' of the title is, of course, Castle's own hostage to fortune, his love for his wife and son, but, like the priest's love for God or Scobie's for the shipwrecked girl Helen Rolt, it is not the only factor. There are two particular moments in *The Heart of the Matter* when Scobie feels happy. The first is just after his wife has left for South Africa, and he takes a stroll in the darkness near his house, towards a Nissen hut which had been unoccupied the day before, but which now has a light in it: 'It seemed to Scobie later that this was the ultimate border he had reached in happiness: being in darkness, alone, with the rain falling, without love or pity' (*HM*, p. 128). One is reminded of Greene's own feelings in Liberia:

And yet all the time, below the fear and the irritation, one was aware of a curious lightness and freedom; one might drink, that was a temporary weakening; but one was happy all the same; one had crossed the boundary into country really strange; surely one had gone deep this time. (*JWM*, p. 132)

One is reminded too of a poem by Samuel Beckett, written in 1948, the year *The Heart of the Matter* was published:

> I would love my love to die
> and the rain to be raining on the graveyard
> and on me walking the streets
> mourning her who thought she loved me.[25]

Scobie's second moment of happiness comes as he leaves the Nissen hut, having found and fallen in love with Helen Rolt inside it: 'He walked away, feeling an extraordinary happiness, but this he would not remember as happiness, as he would remember setting out in the darkness, in the rain, alone' (*HM*, p. 133). Love, companionship, security, are only one kind of happiness – and not necessarily the most satisfying – for Greene's protagonists. The other kind is to be found in darkness, secrecy and loneliness, and, sure enough, lying in bed beside his wife in the ordinary Berkhamsted house, with the Laughing Cavalier over the door, Castle goes in search of it:

> He didn't want to sleep until he was sure from her breathing that Sarah was asleep first. Then he allowed himself to strike, like his childhood hero Allan Quartermain, off on that long slow underground stream which bore him on towards the interior of the dark continent where he hoped that he might find a permanent home, in a city where he could be accepted as a citizen, as a citizen without any pledge of faith, not the City of God or Marx, but the city called Peace of Mind. (*HF*, p. 107)

GREENE AND OTHERS

At the end of *Ways of Escape* there is an epilogue entitled 'The Other', which affectionately parodies Jorge Luis Borges. Borges' own 'other' is, of course, himself – a teasing image of the objective reality which for ever escapes the writer. Greene's is a genuine other, a ne'er-do-well of the Jones/Anthony Farrant variety who sometimes goes under the name of Graham Greene and causes confusion to the press or to friends of the real Greene. The difference is significant. Borges is mentioned in *The Honorary Consul*, where Plarr reads his collection of stories, *Ficciones*, as 'a welcome change from Doctor Saavedra's last novel', since 'Borges shared the tastes he had himself inherited from his father – Conan Doyle, Stevenson, Chesterton' (*HC*, p. 74). But, whereas Borges' response to the adventure stories of his childhood is to transform them into ironic literary artifices, Greene's is to make them serve again as models for experience. Borges dwells on the systems invented by the human mind – theology, philosophy, literature – and succeeds in suggesting at one remove the amorphous and elusive reality behind the systems; Greene is less wary. His stories are not presented as patterns of the mind but as patterns of reality. Yet, since they *are* patterns of the mind and – as this study has tried to show – peculiarly specialized ones, the gap between what they purport to be and what they are grows wider as one gets to know the books better. The reader begins to supply the missing irony for himself – to say, as it were, 'it's only old Greene up to his devil-dance again'; indeed, Greene's retrospective attitude to his own books in *Ways of Escape* and in the introductions to his Collected Edition is somewhat in the same vein.

The obsessive solitariness, even misanthropy, of the protagonists links Greene with Beckett rather than Borges. Again they are presented without irony, as a direct statement of reality, whereas Beckett's solipsists are as hedged with dubiety and fictional devices as Borges' structures. I have already pointed out how the 'transparent' narrator in Anthony Powell's novels allows the characters and events an objectivity denied to Greene's; that transparency, however, is also more and more called into question through the course of Powell's twelve-novel sequence, as meanings and relationships are revealed which were previously missed or misunderstood by the narrator. If one cites a fifth novelist of the same generation, Vladimir Nabokov, whose obsession with his childhood and vision of it as a lost paradise is certainly comparable to Greene's, but whose approach is again oblique and ironic, one begins to see that Greene is the odd man out.

These are all writers born around the turn of the century, all romantics with sheltered childhoods who have had to face up to the twentieth-century failure of the Victorian world-order and the questioning of its values in both public and private terms. Borges and Powell, by their different techniques for neutralizing themselves, have evolved into classicists; Nabokov, driven out of his own country by the revolution, turned Russia into a fairy-tale landscape for ever out of reach and therefore for ever potent as a romantic standard by which to judge his characters' and the world's inadequacy; Beckett, like Greene a rebel against the world that sheltered him and a voluntary exile, retreated into the cave of himself. Only Greene has tried to retain the romantic forms of the old world – including the romantic protagonist and the romantic self within the protagonist – and to use them as the direct expression of a reality which conflicts with the original content of the forms. If it is a bold solution, it is also rather naïve. If it makes things easy for the conservative reader and plays a part in Greene's enormous popularity, it raises increasing problems of credibility as the novels get older and are more objectively analysed.

Romanticism and reality will seem to square with one another only as long as the particular brand of romanticism is shared by the author and his or her public. Once that becomes suspect, or even ludicrous, the work loses its current value and drops away into the past, to be remembered, if at all, only as a forerunner, a historical phenomenon, a book for children or the basis for adaptations to another medium. Some of the work of Buchan, Hope and Haggard, for example – Greene's second-division masters – will survive in this way, in spite of the now embarrassingly 'period' attitudes it enshrines. Clearly Greene's rather too schematic reaction against those attitudes – his substitution in the make-up of his protagonists of weakness, corruption, disloyalty and uncertainty for the strength, integrity, loyalty and self-confidence that characterize Buchan's and Haggard's imperialist heroes – will date in its turn, though for the present it is still sufficiently widely shared by readers and imitated by younger writers to appear normal and therefore realistic. The question is how much will remain when the attitudes have lost their savour. Three things, I suggest, which are perhaps only three aspects of the same thing, guarantee Greene's staying-power.

The first is that behind the attitudes – the authorial *pensées*, the preaching of Javitt and others, the forced similes – Greene does explore real pain and unhappiness and not always solely in his protagonists. The pain is felt through his protagonists, but it is often drawn off the subsidiary characters, the protagonists acting as a kind of central conduit for whatever *Angst* or suffering is around, much in the way that a priest does or is supposed to do. In this sense, one can say that Greene's fiction has a genuine religious dimension, not to be confused with that melodramatic backdrop of good and evil which he used as a way of raising the stakes and laying on the colours.

I am not certain whether Greene himself is fully conscious of this active core in his work – if he were, I suspect he would have formulated it more obviously into a *pensée* or a sermon – but it accounts not only for the powerful effect some of his books have had on those in need of spiritual comfort but also for the ordinary reader's feeling that, for all the mud that can be thrown at the rhetorical style, the over-controlled plots, the morality-play characters and the artificial theology, these are not negligible fictions. Why does the whisky priest in *The Power and the Glory* turn back into danger and sacrifice his life in order to hear a criminal's confession, why is it so appalling that Scobie can't make his confession, why does Fowler in *The Quiet American* wish that there was someone to whom he could say he was sorry for causing Pyle's death? These are not just Catholic quibbles. Even the irreligious Brown wonders whether the happiest moment he and his mistress ever knew was not the time when they trusted each other with mutual self-revelations instead of caresses.

The act of confession, in itself and regardless of its ritual orthodoxy – the sharing of one's pain with someone else – is a movement towards 'the city called Peace of Mind', just as the schoolboy Greene was pulled back from despair by his visit to the psychoanalyst. Yet Scobie and Castle can approach that city only by complete withdrawal into themselves. The tension set up between these two incompatible kinds of happiness – or at least temporary alleviations of unhappiness – is at the heart of *The Heart of the Matter*, as of all Greene's best work. Indeed, it is there in most of his work in some form; only that in the novels which are most likely to outlast the decay of their overt attitudes – *The Heart of the Matter*, *The Power and the Glory*, *The Quiet American*, *The Comedians* – it is tauter and more deeply lodged in the story.

The second thing that makes Greene more than a temporary

73

phenomenon is, paradoxically, what is most contemporary about him: his settings and situations. In spite of its distortions, Greeneland is real. No European writer since Conrad has put the hot, poor and foully governed places of the earth on paper as vividly as Greene. This is not to say that he has described them as they are, from the point of view of God or even of their inhabitants, but as they appeared and smelt and felt and tasted to the European visitor in the middle decades of the twentieth century. Nor are these simply heightened descriptions – or a good travel writer or journalist might have done them as well – but, like Conrad's, they are moral landscapes, characterizations of what is there and of whom it is experienced by. In other words, they contain to a remarkable degree the history and politics of both parties to the encounter. The political part of Greene's plots is fairly standard and even banal – inevitably so, since tyrants, spies, corruption and oppression are hardly newer than human society – but, just as the spiritual element is to be found not in his well-publicized Catholic backdrop but buried deep in his protagonists, so the true political element is intrinsic to his settings and forms a kind of parallel to the spiritual element, for it too involves the tension between apartness and collusion.

The European is safe and in control of himself so long as he keeps the place at arm's length, but the place offers him – and surely it's the reason he came there – loss of control, a temporary unburdening, the opportunity to give and receive. Scobie gives way and then regains control, Querry holds on to himself and then gives way, Brown's is a long process of slipping into collusion with the place, Fowler thrashes to and fro. And of course the fact that, since the days of Conrad, the Europeans have resigned their empires to the United States makes collusion easier for Greene's characters than it was for Conrad's, whose apartness was supported and indeed demanded by a whole society and its patriarchal ethos. From Scobie, who still inhabits a largely Conradian tropic, to Brown and Plarr in their especially squalid pockets of the new American hegemony, Greeneland documents and mythologizes this transitional phase of history, providing the equivalent to Dickens's early industrial London, say, or Chekhov's pre-revolutionary Russia. In so far as the subsidiary characters in Greene's novels have an existence independent of the protagonists, it is as emanations of their political landscapes. To read Greene's novels is to be haunted ever afterwards by places and times with human features or humans who are half made up of places and times. The dentist and the half-caste in *The Power and the Glory* are the ghosts of pre-war Mexico; the two young guards in the roadside watchtower in *The Quiet American* are Vietnam in the last days of the French; Rycker and Deo Gratias in *A Burnt-Out Case* are the Congo when it was still Belgian, and so on.

The third thing takes us back to the *pensée* with which this study began. In a generation or two, if it doesn't already, this kind of detachable sentiment, which can be put into the mouth of any protagonist, will sound as quaint as some of Richard Hannay's sentiments. But in that the protagonists' self-examinations, however slickly expressed, reflect those of a man who could never forgive or forget the process of growing up, they will continue to have meaning: not just for students of the particular author Graham Greene, but for any reader trapped in that narrow but sometimes lifelong defile leading from dependence and immaturity to responsibility for one's own actions and the happiness of others. It is one of the central themes of literature, especially of English literature, and although it may have been handled with broader sympathy and deeper understanding by the greatest writers – including Greene's own first-division masters, James and Conrad – it has never been done with more intimate passion than by Greene.

NOTES

1 Barbara Greene, *Too Late to Turn Back* (London: Settle & Bendall, 1981), p. 6. (Originally published as *Land Benighted* (London: Geoffrey Bles, 1938).)

2 Graham Greene, *Three Plays* (London: Mercury Books, 1961), p. 93.

3 Graham Greene, *British Dramatists* (London: Collins, 1942), p. 13.

4 Ibid., p. 19.

5 Ibid., p. 8.

6 Ibid., p. 19.

7 Ibid., p. 38.

8 T. S. Eliot, *Collected Poems 1909–35* (London: Faber, 1936), pp. 63 and 69. Eliot quotes Webster to darken his picture of the 'unreal City'.

9 Graham Greene, *The Pleasure Dome*, ed. John Russell Taylor (London: Oxford University Press, 1980), p. 142.

10 Richard Hoggart, 'The Force of Caricature', in *Speaking to Each Other* (London: Oxford University Press/Chatto & Windus, 1970), pp. 40–55; repr. in Samuel Hynes (ed.), *Graham Greene: A Collection of Critical Essays* (Englewood Cliffs, NJ: Prentice-Hall, 1973), p. 91.

11 George Orwell, 'The Sanctified Sinner, in *The Collected Essays, Journalism and Letters of George Orwell*, ed. Sonia Orwell and Ian Angus (New York and London: Harcourt Brace Jovanovich and Secker & Warburg, 1968), pp. 439–43; repr. in Hynes (ed.), op. cit., p. 107.

12 Interview with Gene D. Phillips, 'Graham Greene: On the Screen', *The Catholic World*, 209 (August 1969), pp. 218–21; repr. in Hynes (ed.), op. cit., p. 175.

13 Interview with Philip French in *Graham Greene at 75*, broadcast on BBC Radio 3, 1 October 1979.

14 'The Job of the Writer', *The Observer*, 15 September 1957.

15 John Atkins, *Graham Greene*, 2nd edn (London: Calder & Boyars, 1966), p. 194.

16 Frank Kermode, 'Mr Greene's Eggs and Crosses', in *Puzzles and Epiphanies* (London: Routledge & Kegan Paul, 1962; New York: Chilmark Press, 1963), pp. 176–87; repr. in Hynes (ed.), op. cit., pp. 133 and 137.

17 *Graham Greene at 75*, broadcast on BBC Radio 3, 1 October 1979.

18 Ibid.

19 Graham Greene, *Three Plays*, p. 166.

20 Graham Greene, *The Return of A. J. Raffles* (Harmondsworth: Penguin, 1975), p. 39.

21 Graham Greene, *The Pleasure Dome*, pp. 60–1.

22 Hoggart, op. cit., in Hynes (ed.), op. cit., pp. 84–5.

23 Ibid., p. 92.

24 At the front of *The Lawless Roads* Greene places a long quotation from Cardinal Newman which ends: 'either there is no Creator, or this living society of men is in a true sense discarded from His presence . . . *if* there be a God, *since* there is a God, the human race is implicated in some terrible aboriginal calamity.'

25 Samuel Beckett, *Poems in English* (London: John Calder, 1961), p. 53.

BIBLIOGRAPHY

WORKS BY GRAHAM GREENE

All Greene's books are available in the hardback Collected Edition (London: Heinemann/Bodley Head) and in paperback (Harmondsworth: Penguin) unless otherwise stated. The American Uniform Edition is published by Viking Press, New York. The books are listed below with their original dates of publication.

Novels

The Man Within. 1929.
The Name of Action. London: Heinemann, 1930. Garden City, NY: Doubleday, 1930. (Not in paperback.)
Rumour at Nightfall. London: Heinemann, 1931. Garden City, NY: Doubleday, 1931. (Not in paperback.)
Stamboul Train. 1932.
It's a Battlefield. 1934.
England Made Me. 1935.
A Gun for Sale (US title: *This Gun for Hire*). 1936.
Brighton Rock. 1938.
The Confidential Agent. 1939.
The Power and the Glory. 1940.
The Ministry of Fear. 1943.
The Heart of the Matter. 1948.
The Third Man/The Fallen Idol. 1950. (*The Fallen Idol* was originally published as 'The Basement Room' in 1935 and later included in *Nineteen Stories* (1947) and *Twenty-One Stories* (1954).)
The End of the Affair. 1951.
Loser Takes All. 1955.
The Quiet American. 1955.
Our Man in Havana. 1958.
A Burnt-Out Case. 1961.
The Comedians. 1966.
Travels with my Aunt. 1969.

The Honorary Consul. 1973.

The Human Factor. 1978.

Doctor Fischer of Geneva, or The Bomb Party. London: Bodley Head, 1980.

Monsignor Quixote. London: Bodley Head, 1982. (Not in paperback.)

Short stories

Twenty-One Stories (first published in 1947 as *Nineteen Stories*). 1954.

A Sense of Reality. 1963.

May We Borrow Your Husband? 1967.

Travel

Journey Without Maps. 1936.

The Lawless Roads. 1939.

In Search of a Character. 1961.

Essays

The Pleasure Dome: The Collected Film Criticism 1935–40. Ed. John Russell Taylor. London: Secker & Warburg, 1972. London: Oxford University Press, 1980 (paperback).

British Dramatists. London: Collins, 1942. (Not in paperback. Repr. in *The Heritage of British Literature* (London: Thames & Hudson, 1983).)

Collected Essays. 1969.

Plays

The Living Room. London: Heinemann, 1953. (Not in paperback.)

The Potting Shed. London: Heinemann, 1958.

The Complaisant Lover. London: Heinemann, 1959. (Not in paperback.)

Three Plays. London: Mercury Books, 1961 (paperback). (Includes *The Living Room, The Potting Shed* and *The Complaisant Lover.*)

Carving a Statue. London: Bodley Head, 1964.

The Return of A. J. Raffles. London: Bodley Head, 1975.

Autobiography

A Sort of Life. 1971.

Ways of Escape. London: Bodley Head, 1980.
(This book is partly made up of the introductions to the Collected Edition.)

Allain, Marie-Françoise. *The Other Man: Conversations with Graham Greene*. London: The Bodley Head, 1983. (Not in paperback.)

Biography

Lord Rochester's Monkey. London: Bodley Head, 1974. London: Futura, 1976 (paperback). (This book was written 1931–4, but refused publication at the time.)

Pamphlet

J'Accuse – The Dark Side of Nice. London: Bodley Head, 1982.

BIBLIOGRAPHY

Vann, J. Don. *Graham Greene: A Checklist of Criticism*. Kent, Ohio: Kent State University Press, 1970.

SELECTED CRITICISM OF GRAHAM GREENE

Allott, Kenneth, and Farris, Miriam. *The Art of Graham Greene*. London: Hamish Hamilton, 1951.

Atkins, John. *Graham Greene*. London: Calder & Boyars, 1957. 2nd edn 1966.

Boardman, Gwenn R. *Graham Greene: The Aesthetics of Exploration*. Gainesville, Fla.: University of Florida Press, 1971.

De Vitis, A. A. *Graham Greene*. New York: Twayne, 1964.

Evans, Robert O. (ed.). *Graham Greene: Some Critical Considerations*. Lexington, Ky: University of Kentucky Press, 1963.

Hynes, Samuel (ed.). *Graham Greene: A Collection of Critical Essays*. Englewood Cliffs, NJ: Prentice-Hall, 1973.

Kulshrestha, J. P. *Graham Greene: The Novelist*. New Delhi: Macmillan, 1977.

Kunkel, Francis L. *The Labyrinthine Ways of Graham Greene*. New York: Sheed & Ward, 1959.

Lodge, David. *Graham Greene*. New York and London: Columbia University Press, 1966.

Pryce-Jones, David. *Graham Greene*. Edinburgh: Oliver & Boyd, 1963. 2nd edn 1973.

Stratford, Philip. *Faith and Fiction: Creative Process in Greene and Mauriac*. Notre Dame, Ind.: University of Notre Dame Press, 1964.

Wolfe, Peter. *Graham Greene the Entertainer*. Carbondale and Edwardsville, Ill.: Southern Illinois University Press, 1972. London and Amsterdam: Feffer & Simons, 1972.

Wyndham, Francis. *Graham Greene*. London: Longmans, Green, 1955.